SUNDAY TELEGRAPH

101 WAYS OF SAVING TAX

SUNDAY TELEGRAPH

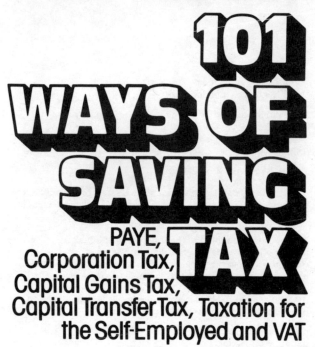

101 WAYS OF SAVING TAX

PAYE, Corporation Tax, Capital Gains Tax, Capital Transfer Tax, Taxation for the Self-Employed and VAT

Touche Ross & Co

Published by the Sunday Telegraph
135 Fleet Street, London EC4P 4BL

First published April 1982
© Touche Ross & Co. 1983
Second edition, updated, March 1983
ISBN 0 901684 93 7

Design by Martin Bronkhorst

Printed in Great Britain by
Biddles Ltd, Guildford.
Typeset by Sunset Phototype Ltd, Barnet.

Preface

This book has become as much a part of the tax season as that awful tax form that arrives in the spring. When I first read the manuscript prepared by the tax specialists of Touche Ross in 1980, it seemed a natural for Sunday Telegraph readers and in January 1981 we published our first edition. It was a sell-out.

Since then we have updated it to take account of the changes in the 1981 and 1982 Finance Acts, and this latest edition updates it again to take account of the substantial changes in Sir Geoffrey's latest – and quite possible his last – Budget. It is quite conceivable of course that there could be further changes before the Finance Bill becomes law, particularly if there is an early election. But I promise you this – at the time this first arrives in the book shops, it is as up-to-date as it is possible to make it, and certainly at least as up-to-date as anything else on the market.

For new readers let me briefly set out the object and the thought behind *101 Ways of Saving Tax*: it is written by two leading tax specialists, Elaine Baker and Bill Packer of Touche Ross. They have distilled their knowledge and experience into a form and language which is as simple as tax can possibly be. It has one object only: to save you money. There are many simple, perfectly legal and straightforward ways whereby almost any taxpayer can pay less tax. Here we set them out in a way that any taxpayer will understand – and, it the reaction to previous editions is anything to go by, will appreciate.

Ivan Fallon, City Editor, March 1983

Contents

*Indicates 1983 Budget changes.
See Budget Appendix page 135.

	I Basic Questions for the Individual (Income Tax)	*Page*
* 1	Do I have to pay tax? If so, how much will I have to pay?	1
* 2	Is there any extra tax to pay on my investment income?	3
* 3	When and how do I pay the tax? What can I do if I disagree with the amount I am asked to pay?	4
4	Can I save tax by keeping quiet?	6
* 5	What is the basic personal allowance?	7
* 6	Can I claim for my wife and children?	8
7	Are there any other personal allowances I can claim for myself or my family?	8
8	What happens to my tax in the year of my marriage?	10
* 9	If I am a working wife do I pay my own tax?	10
10	Can I be separately assessed from my husband? Do I have to pay my wife's tax?	11
*11	What happens if our marriage comes to an end?	14
12	If I am a single parent family what can I claim?	17
13	Can I claim tax relief on my life assurance premiums?	18
*14	How can I prepare for my retirement?	18
*15	What National Insurance contributions should I pay?	21

✳16 If I am over 65 years of age, do I still pay tax?   22

17 Are all Social Security benefits taxable?   23

✳18 What income tax reliefs can I claim in respect of my home?   24

19 What other loan interest can I claim?   25

20 Do I pay tax on my bank interest?   27

21 Where should I invest my capital?   27

✳22 Can a deed of covenant save me tax?   30

23 Can I set aside money towards my taxes?   34

24 I have other sources of income which are not taxed at source: how are they taxed?   35

25 If I have income subject to overseas taxation can I get any relief in the United Kingdom?   35

✳26 What happens when I die?   36

II You've Earned it (Taxation of the Employee)

27 What is included in my earnings for income tax purposes and how are they taxed under the PAYE system?   38

28 If I pay tax under PAYE will I also be assessed at the end of each year? If so, how will I be assessed?   40

29 How much can I receive tax free when I cease my employment?   43

30 Are perks taxable?   44

31 What is my tax position if I have a company car, or use my own car for business purposes?   46

32 I have always lived in this country but part of my work is now done abroad: can I claim any tax relief?   47

33 I have always lived abroad but now I have come to work in the United Kingdom: what is my tax position?   51

34 Are there any other expenses I can claim?   52

III Now You're in Business (Taxation of the Self-Employed)

35 What happens when I start up in business? 54
36 How do I choose my accounting date? 55
37 What happens if I change my accounting date? 57
38 What happens when my business ceases? 57
39 What can I do if I incur a loss in the first years of trading? 58
40 What other ways are there of relieving losses? 59
✱41 What can I claim as expenses? 61
42 What is the effect for tax purposes of capital expenditure? 63
43 What is the tax position on buying motor cars? If I use my own car can I claim tax allowances? 66
44 What is the tax effect of increases or decreases in my year end stock valuations? 67
45 Are there any deductions that I can claim which apply more to self-employment rather than if I am an employee? 69
46 Are there any businesses which have special rules? 71
47 What is the position if I am in partnership? 72
48 What happens if there is a change in the partnership? 74
49 Part of my business is carried on abroad: can I claim any tax deduction for this? 74
50 Should I consider turning my business into a company? 76
51 What are the advantages and disadvantages of incorporating my business? 77
52 How does incorporation actually affect my income tax position? 78

IV Keeping Good Company (Taxation of the Company — Corporation Tax)

✳ 53 What are the basic rules of corporation tax (including rates of tax, reliefs, dates for payments, special rules, etc.)?   79

54 What are the profits of a company? Are they computed in the same way as for income tax?   81

55 What are charges on income and how are they dealt with?   82

56 Can my company claim stock relief in the same way as an individual or partnership?   82

57 Can my company claim allowances for capital expenditure in the same way as an individual or partnership?   82

58 If my company incurs losses, how can they be utilised?   83

✳ 59 As a director of the company, is there any advantage in reducing the profit by drawing more remuneration?   83

60 What is the capital gains tax position of a company?   84

✳ 61 What are the tax consequences if my company pays a dividend?   85

62 When and why is a receiver or liquidator appointed to a company?   88

63 What happens if a receiver is appointed to my company?   89

64 What happens if a liquidator is appointed?   90

65 Should my company stay on its own or become a member of a group?   91

✳ 66 Can I set up a company overseas and what would be the tax position?   92

V Some You Win – Some You Lose (Capital Gains Tax and the Individual)

❋67 What is capital gains tax? What are the rates of tax and do I still pay capital gains tax if my gains are not substantial? 95

68 Are any assets exempt from this tax? 97

69 Is my home a chargeable asset? 98

70 What is my position if I own more than one property? 99

❋71 Does it make any difference if I let my house or take paying guests? 100

72 How am I affected if I use part of my house as an office? 101

73 Are gifts chargeable to capital gains tax? 101

❋74 If I make a gift which is not exempt from capital gains tax, is there any relief I can claim? 102

75 Can I save tax by claiming expenses? 103

❋76 If I make a capital loss, can I turn this to my advantage? 103

77 What is a bed and breakfast transaction? 105

❋78 If I am married, how does this affect my capital gains position? 106

79 I have assets which I acquired before capital gains tax was introduced (on 6th April 1965). What is the position on these? 107

80 What are paper for paper transactions and how do they affect my capital gains position? 109

❋81 Are there any other reliefs for which I may qualify in certain circumstances? 110

82 When do I pay my capital gains tax, and are there any other administrative details I should know? 112

VI Capital Ways of Saving Tax (Capital Transfer Tax)

✳83 What is capital transfer tax? What are the rates of tax and when am I liable to pay it?   113

84 Does it make any difference where I live?   115

85 Can I make a transfer without it being a transfer of value?   116

86 Who pays the tax on a chargeable transfer?   116

✳87 When is the tax payable and is there any way to delay payment?   117

88 What are the alternatives if I do not have the necessary funds available to pay the tax?   118

89 Can I make gifts without adding to my cumulative chargeable transfers?   119

✳90 Apart from the gifts mentioned in question 89, are there any other exempt transfers I can make?   120

91 What is excluded property?   122

✳92 If I have made chargeable transfers, are there any reliefs I can claim?   123

93 How is my estate calculated at my death and are there any further reliefs my personal representatives can claim?   125

94 How are my assets valued?   125

95 Is it possible to change arrangements made by a will after the death has taken place, and if so, what are the tax consequences?   127

96 If I create a settlement, will I pay more tax; will the trust also be liable to pay capital transfer tax? If so, are there any trusts which are exempt?   128

97 If I am a trustee, and must therefore pay the tax, are there any reliefs I can claim?   129

VII The Indirect Tax You Must Pay (Value Added Tax)

✱98 When do I have to register for VAT and is
there any tax planning to consider?   130

✱99 If I am registered for VAT, what happens if
there is a change in my circumstances?   131

100 Is there any way I can plan to minimise the
tax charge and are there any special rules if
my business is a company?   132

VIII Range of Possibilities

✱101 A final word   133

IX Special 1983 Budget Supplement and Checklist
Contains *all* the March 1983 Budget changes.   135

I
Basic Questions for the Individual
INCOME TAX

Do I have to pay tax? If so, how much will I have to pay? 　　1 ✳

You may be amused to learn that, in theory, income tax is only a temporary measure; it has to be renewed by Parliament each year, and will cease to be imposed by Parliament when the country no longer requires revenue to be raised in this manner! Income tax was first introduced in 1799 to pay for the Napoleonic wars, and was abolished after Waterloo, in 1816. In 1842, income tax was reintroduced by Sir Robert Peel, again as a temporary measure, but well over a century later income tax is still being paid!

The United Kingdom is one of the higher taxed countries of the world, and as it also has one of the most complicated tax systems, it is important that you understand what your *taxable income* is.

The total income of you, as an individual, should include income of both yourself and your wife (if applicable), from all sources whether earned or unearned. *Earned income* is income arising from any office or employment, the personal carrying-on of a trade, profession or vocation, pay or pension in respect of past services, and certain social security benefits. *Investment* (or *unearned*) income includes dividends plus tax credits, property income, interest from banks or building societies, annual payments etc. (NB: these lists are not exhaustive.)

To arrive at your taxable income, from this total figure is deducted allowances, reliefs and charges on income (covered in later questions); the latter includes annual payments and interest paid which is allowable for tax purposes. Charges are normally deducted from investment income first, unless it is advantageous for you to have the deduction from your earned income first.

Having arrived at the figure of your taxable income, this is taxed according to the income tax rates for that particular year. A year, for income tax purposes, commences on *6th April*, so the references to the end of a tax year are to *5th April*, not 31st December. The current tax year, *1982/83, runs from 6th April 1982 to 5th April 1983* and the rates that are applied to your taxable income are as shown below:

Rate	Taxable income
%	£
30	1 – 12,800
40	12,801 – 15,100
45	15,101 – 19,100
50	19,101 – 25,300
55	25,301 – 31,500
60	over 31,500

The following example shows how the amount of taxable income is arrived at and how the tax is charged.

Example

Stan D. Easy is a retired army corporal and in the current year 1982/83 he receives an annual pension of £2,500; he is now in part-time employment and receives a salary of £4,000 per annum. He holds shares in many companies and during the year ended 5th April 1983 he receives dividends plus tax credits of £3,000. He pays mortgage interest on his house of £1,015, and he is a married man – his wife's only income is interest from a bank account amounting to £30.

His taxable income is as follows:

		£
Salary		4,000
Pension		2,500
Dividends + tax credits		3,000
Bank interest (wife) (see question 20)		30
Total income		9,530
less Interest paid		1,015
		8,515
less Personal allowance (see question 6)		2,445
Taxable income		£6,070

This is charged to tax at 30%: £6,070 @ 30% = £1,821.00. Stan's total tax bill is therefore £1,821.00. From this figure is deducted all the tax he has paid and it is then possible to see whether he has paid too much or too little tax during the year, the balance being either collected from him, or repaid to him (see also question 3).

Is there any extra tax to pay on my investment income? 2✱

If your unearned income exceeds a specified limit (for 1982/83 this is £6,250), you will have to pay an *investment income surcharge* of 15% on the excess of your unearned income over that limit, following any deduction for charges which may be applicable. If this additional charge applies to your investment income, you may like to consider ways in which it can be reduced (see question 21).

Commonly, investment income is paid with income tax at the basic rate deducted at source. If therefore you are liable to tax at the higher rate (including the investment income surcharge) it will be necessary for the Inspector of Taxes to issue a special assessment (known as a "taxed income" assessment) to collect the additional liability. This additional tax is not due for payment until 1st December following the end of the year of assessment concerned, at the earliest: thus the additional liability for 1982/83 will not be due for payment until 1st December 1983. If the assessment is not issued in time for the 1st December due date the tax then becomes due 30 days after the notice of assessment is issued.

✳3 **When and how do I pay the tax? What can I do if I disagree with the amount I am asked to pay?**

Tax will be collected from you in one of two ways – either by *deduction at source* or by way of an *assessment* issued by the Inspector of Taxes, which informs you of the amount to pay direct to the Revenue.

The most common example of tax being deducted at source is if you are an employee – you will receive your weekly/monthly salary after tax and national insurance contributions have been deducted (see also question 27). On the other hand you may be a self-employed person, in which case there is no employer to deduct tax from your earnings during the tax year. Instead, you will send in accounts to the Inspector of Taxes showing details of your income and expenditure for the year and he will then issue an assessment on your taxable profit for the relevant tax year (see also questions 35 to 52). Unearned income is also taxed by assessment unless it is a very small amount, in which case part of your personal allowances will be used to cover the amount chargeable. There is yet another form of assessment, to collect higher rate tax and the investment income surcharge due on investment income (see question 2). Finally, even if you are an employee you may receive an assessment (which will show income from employments and the tax deducted) after the end of the tax year if, for some reason, you have paid too much or too little tax, despite the regular deductions made by your employer (see question 28 for more details).

For whatever reason you receive an assessment you should always check to see if it is correct. If you have a professional adviser you should authorise him to receive a copy of all assessments issued to you. If for some reason you are not prepared to do this, you *must* give him your own copy of the notice of assessment as soon as possible.

If you do not agree with the figures shown on the assessment you have 30 days in which to *appeal* against it, stating your reasons and whether or not you wish part, or all, of the tax charged to be withheld from collection until the figures have been agreed. The procedure for making an appeal or a request for postponement of the tax charged, is covered in the notes which are always issued with a notice of assessment, but if you have a professional adviser he will deal with this for you.

If you appeal against an assessment on the grounds that it is estimated and the Inspector of Taxes is awaiting accounts or other details from you, you should not delay sending him the information – he has the right to take you before an independent body called the General Commissioners who, when the facts are put before them, have the power to determine (or confirm) the assessment in whatever amount they consider appropriate, which almost inevitably leads to excessive tax having to be paid by you!

If you are self-employed you will normally pay the tax due in two equal instalments on *1st January* during the year of assessment and *1st July* immediately following the end of the year of assessment. For the year 1982/83 tax is payable on 1st January 1983 and 1st July 1983 (remembering that the year commences on 6th April 1982 and ends on 5th April 1983). If the assessment is issued too late to pay tax on these dates you will be given *30 days* to pay the tax.

If there is tax to pay on an assessment, *the notice will always state quite clearly the due date for payment of the tax. Remember* there is an *interest charge* (currently at 12% per annum) which accrues daily from what is called the *reckonable date* (which will vary depending on the circumstances) to the date payment of the tax is made.

You should not delay paying your tax after the due and payable date — it will benefit no-one, for you always run the risk of having an extra charge to pay — interest. If you incur an interest charge on overdue tax (of any description) it is not deductible for *any* tax purposes.

On the other hand, if the situation is reversed and the Inland Revenue owe you a refund of tax, there may be a repayment supplement due to you. Again, this is calculated at 12% per annum and will be paid to you providing certain tests concerning original due dates of payment of the tax are fulfilled.

---

4   Can I save tax by keeping quiet?

A surprising number of people think that if they do not send in their income tax returns or trading accounts it will save them tax. There are also a number of people who omit, quite inadvertently, to make entries on their returns of income, or neglect to keep the Revenue informed of their circumstances. Finally, there are the people who deliberately withhold information from the Inland Revenue in the belief that no-one will ever know, and they have therefore "got away with it"!

These people are, of course, quite wrong in their views – there is no excuse for withholding details of your income and gains from the Inland Revenue. Even if the Inspector fails to send you an income tax return for completion, this does not discharge you from liability – you should inform him even if he does not ask. Be certain *you* are not misled into thinking "the Inspector will never know" – the Revenue has extensive powers which are used to obtain information not only from you as an individual, but from any other sources.

The most common source from which the Revenue receives information is the banks who, by law, have to forward to the Revenue, details of interest credited to each person's deposit account. This information is imparted to the individual's own tax office and checked with his return . . . the rest is obvious! This is just an example but in the large cases of omission from returns etc. there can be *interest charges* and *penalties*, in addition to the tax charged, possibly for many years of assessment.

The answer then to this question is most definitely – *no*. Instead of paying *less* tax you *may end up paying large amounts of tax in lump sums, penalties, interest* and possibly a *professional adviser's fee* if you employed someone to deal with your problems.

What is the basic personal allowance?   5 ✷

For 1982/83 the *lower* personal allowance is £1,565. This will be granted if you are an unmarried person (whether single, divorced or widowed), and even if you are not entitled to claim any other allowances, this amount will be deducted from your income before the tax is calculated.

Legislation was introduced in 1980 for indexation of the main personal allowances (including this relief) so the amount of relief should be revised each tax year, by reference to any increase in the retail price index during the 12 months to the previous December. The amounts of the increase will be rounded up to the nearest £100. Indexation, was not applied to the allowances for 1981/82, which remained unchanged from 1980/81.

The allowances for the current year 1982/83 have however been increased by 2% above the amount necessary to keep pace with the level of inflation.

✳6   Can I claim for my wife and children?

There is a *higher* personal allowance due if you are a married man and your wife lives with you, or is wholly maintained by you. There are special rules for the year of marriage or separation (see questions 8 and 11). The relief for 1982/83 is £2,445.

Tax allowances in respect of children were abolished recently, except for certain children living abroad and for certain students over 19 years of age. The allowances have been replaced by child benefits which are payable direct to the mother of the child by the Department of Health and Social Security normally through the Post Office. These child benefits are not taxable.

It should be pointed out that the status of a common law wife is not recognised for tax purposes.

---

7   Are there any other personal allowances I can claim for myself or my family?

There are several other reliefs which you may be able to claim; these are noted below:

Dependent Relatives: The dependant must be a relative who is maintained by the claimant, and must be incapacitated by old age or infirmity, unless it is the mother of the claimant, or his wife, when the only test is that she is widowed, divorced or separated. ("Relative" includes relatives of husband and wife.)

The allowance is £100 a year but this is increased to £145 for a woman claimant other than a married woman living with her husband. To obtain the full allowance the relative's income must not exceed the basic retirement pension for the year in question – the allowance is reduced by £1 for every £1 the relative's income exceeds this limit.

If the relative is not living with you, the allowance will be given, as a concession, if your contribution is £75 or more each year.

An allowance may be claimed for *each* dependent relative.

Daughter's or Son's Services: The daughter or son must be resident with the claimant and be maintained by him. He must be compelled to depend on their services because of old age or infirmity. The allowance is £55 a year.

Blind Person's Relief: This can be claimed by a single person or a married man if he (or his wife) is registered as blind throughout the whole or part of the year. If both spouses are blind, the allowance is given twice. The allowance is £360 a year.

Housekeeper Allowance: A claim for this allowance (£100) can be made by a *widow* or *widower* but *not* by a person who is divorced or separated, in respect of a relative who is resident with the claimant, or an unrelated person who is resident and employed as a housekeeper. This is no longer a common relief because if there are children involved there is an additional personal allowance that may be claimed (see question 12).

8   What happens to my tax in the year of my marriage?

As already mentioned under question 1, the income of husband and wife are normally treated as one and taxed accordingly. However in the year of marriage, special rules apply.

At one time, the date of your wedding made a considerable difference to your tax for the year of marriage, if care was taken when choosing the date! Over the years the rules have progressively changed until they now operate as follows:

Husband: The married man's allowance is reduced by one twelfth of the difference between the single and married man's allowances, for each month in the tax year which ended before his marriage (i.e. ending 5th May, 5th June etc.).

Wife: The single person's allowance is given throughout the year of marriage and the wife is not treated as married until 6th April following the date of marriage (i.e. the start of the new tax year). At this point the wife's personal allowances disappear, though if she is working it is replaced by the *Wife's Earned Income Allowance* (see question 9).

✳9   If I am a working wife do I pay my own tax?

As you have already seen, if you are a married woman, for income tax purposes your income is *deemed to be that of your husband*. He must therefore declare all your income (whether it is earned or unearned) on his income tax return and any assessments to be made on your income will be sent direct to him, unless an election has been made to the contrary (see question 10). Your husband is therefore liable to pay the income tax due on your joint incomes (except in special circumstances when the Revenue may require payment from you, or where an election has been made).

The exception to this is if you are employed and pay tax under PAYE. In this case the tax is deducted direct from your earnings and if at the end of the year you have paid too much tax, the repayment will be sent direct to you and not your husband.

As a working wife you will be granted *Wife's Earned Income Allowance* which is the same as the single person's allowance (currently £1,565); if you are self-employed this allowance will be given in the assessment (whether you are trading on your own or in partnership) and if you are employed, the allowance will form the basis for your code number (see question 27). If your earnings are below the amount of the allowance the remainder of the relief has to be forfeited but, *if your husband's income is less than his total allowances, you may claim the excess allowances* against your own income.

Remember this only works one way, the allowances being passed from husband to wife but *not* vice versa.

Can I be separately assessed from my husband? Do I have to   10 pay my wife's tax?

These two questions must be dealt with together as the answers are related: *as the wife – yes,* you can be separately assessed from your husband, and *as the husband – no,* you do not always have to pay your wife's tax.

There are two forms of separate assessment and they must not be confused:

1 Separate taxation of wife's earnings: This is generally called Wife's Earnings Election and works in the following way. It has already been seen that the wife's income is assessed as an additional source of the husband's income and he will pay tax accordingly. If his earnings are very high he may have used up all the basic rate band (which taxes income at 30%) and the wife's income is therefore taxed at 40% or higher. However, the Wife's Earnings Election, *which must be made jointly by husband and wife* during the period from 6 months before until 12 months after the end of the relevant year of assessment, provides that the *wife's earned income becomes her own responsibility*. The husband continues to be assessed on his own income and any income of his wife which is unearned; he *forfeits the higher personal allowance* of a married man and receives only the single person's allowance. The wife is also taxed as a single person, receiving the lower personal allowance, but this way, *both parties receive the benefit of the basic rate band*.

Your joint earnings must be substantial to make a claim worthwhile, remembering that the husband will lose part of his allowances. You should certainly consider making an election if your joint earned income is in the region of £19,000 or more, but the precise level at which it would be advantageous for you personally to make such a claim must depend on your individual circumstances.

In some cases, the Revenue may advise you to make an election, or you should seek professional advice if you are not sure what to do. The election can be revoked, if both parties agree, up to 12 months after the end of the tax year to which the election is no longer to apply.

Example
Paul Over is a director of a knitwear manufacturing company, and in the current tax year 1982/83 he is paid a salary of £17,000 per annum. His wife Eileen D. Over is a keep-fit instructress earning a salary of £6,000 per annum.

Without Wife's Earnings Election tax is due as follows:

	Total £	Paul £	Eileen £
Salary	23,000	17,000	6,000
less allowances:			
Married man's allowance	(2,445)	(2,445)	
Wife's earned income allowance	(1,565)		(1,565)
	18,990	14,555	4,435
Chargeable to tax:			
@ 30%	12,800	12,800	
@ 40%	2,300	1,755	545
@ 45%	3,890		3,890
	18,990	14,555	4,435
Tax due:	£6,510	£4,542	£1,968

With Wife's Earnings Election tax is due as follows:

Salary	23,000	17,000	6,000
less single person's allowance	(3,130)	(1,565)	(1,565)
	19,870	15,435	4,435
Chargeable to tax:			
@ 30%	17,235	12,800	4,435
@ 40%	2,300	2,300	
@ 45%	335	335	
	19,870	15,435	4,435
Tax due:	£6,240	£4,910	£1330

Overall tax saving £ 270

NB: the tax saving would be greater in this example if the wife's salary was higher.

2 Separate assessment of wife's income: Under this arrangement the overall tax position of you as a couple is *not* affected, but the application for this form of separate assessment results in the apportionment of the total tax payable between husband and wife, in proportion to your respective incomes. *The application may be made by either party to the marriage* within six months before 6th July falling in the year of assessment for which these provisions are to apply. There is the same time limit for revoking the election which must be done by the same spouse who originally made the election.

There is *no tax advantage in this form of separate assessment;* however, there are benefits in that the husband may no longer be required to make a return of his wife's income, since if she so wishes she may make her own return. Each person is liable to pay their own income tax and will receive individual assessment. On the other hand if there is a repayment of tax due, that will also be sent to the appropriate individual.

✳11   What happens if our marriage comes to an end?

For income tax purposes there are three ways in which a marriage can come to an end: *separation*, *divorce* or *death*. Technically the marriage is said to have ended when the parties "cease living together" as man and wife. Separation can be formalised by a court order or by deed, but the term also covers the situation where the couple have separated in such circumstances that the separation is likely to be permanent, in which case a formal judicial separation order is not required.

If your marriage should come to an end, it will have the following effect on your income tax:

Husband: You will be allowed the married man's allowance for the whole of the tax year in which the marriage comes to an end (it is not apportioned as in the year of marriage), and from the following 5th April you will be taxed as a single man.

Wife: You will be treated as two separate people to and from the date the marriage comes to an end: before that date you will be given the wife's earned income allowance (if applicable) and your income will be deemed to be that of your husband. From the date of separation or death etc., you will be taxed as a single person, being given the single person's allowance.

If the marriage has ended because of separation or divorce it is quite likely there will be some form of maintenance payable by the husband in respect of his wife, their children, or both. It may be that the separation is amicable, in which case the husband may be making voluntary payments to maintain the family. If he is considered by the Revenue to be wholly maintaining his wife (taking into account any other income she receives) he will continue to be given the married man's personal allowance. If this is the case, the payments are not treated as the wife's income for tax purposes.

For payments made under a court order, it is important to distinguish between a court order made in favour of the wife, which is her income; an order for the payments to be made to the wife for the maintenance of the children, which is also her income; and an order made in favour of the children direct, which is then the child's income. *If the payments are made direct to the children, each child will be granted the single person's allowance.*

Payments made under a court order may be *small maintenance payments* if they do not exceed £33 per week or £143 per month. The payments are made gross with a tax allowance being given for the same amount to the payer. The payments are taxable in the hands of the recipient but although it is a source of unearned income all maintenance payments are specifically exempted from the investment income surcharge (see question 2).

There can also be payments made under a court order from which tax is deducted at source. This means that the husband deducts tax at the basic rate from the gross payments and pays only the net amount to his wife. The payments are treated as a charge on his income and can give relief at both the basic and higher rates of tax, as can be seen from the following example. The payments may also provide a repayment of income tax for the wife if her income is low.

Example

The marriage of Peter Out came to an end several years ago. He is ordered to pay his wife £2,000 each year, before deduction of tax. For 1982/83 his only income is earnings of £17,665.

If he was not paying maintenance, his liability to tax would be as follows:

	£
Income	17,665
less single person's allowance	1,565
Taxable income	16,100
Charged as follows:	
£12,800 @ 30%	3,840
£2,300 @ 40%	920
£1,000 @ 45%	450
Total tax due:	5,210

The actual tax suffered is reduced as follows, taking the £2,000 payment into consideration:

	£
Income	17,665
less maintenance payment	2,000
	15,665
less single person's allowance	1,565
	14,100
Charged as follows	
£12,800 @ 30%	3,840
£1,300 @ 40%	520
Net tax suffered:	4,360

This gives an overall saving of £850, which is made up of £600 retained out of the maintenance payments (not actually paid over to the Revenue) and £250 reduction in higher rate tax liability.

The maintenance payment has therefore had the effect of *increasing the amount charged at the basic rate* by £2,000 and *reducing the amount charged at higher rates* by £2,000. Obviously, the higher the rate of tax, the more relief is obtained. The wife will have received the net amount (£2,000 less tax of £600) and if this is her only income she may reclaim some or all of the tax of £600 depending on what reliefs or deductions she can claim herself.

Note that if the husband has unearned income, maintenance payments are treated as applied against this before his earned income, so possibly reducing his liability to investment income surcharge (see question 2).

If I am a single parent family what can I claim?   12 ✱

There is an additional allowance which may be claimed if you are a person (either male or female) who is not entitled to the married man's allowance, but you have children in your care. The amount of the allowance at present is £880 (the difference between the lower and higher personal allowances), and this is given *once only* irrespective of the number of children involved. If the allowance is being claimed following separation or divorce and both parents claim they are maintaining the children the allowance can be apportioned between them. The child *must be a child of the claimant or if not, must be under 18 and maintained for the whole of the year at the claimant's expense.* In any event the child must be born during the year of assessment or be under 16 at the commencement of the year of assessment; alternatively the child may be over 16 and undergoing full-time instruction at a recognised educational establishment, or undergoing training by an employer, for not less than two years, for a trade, profession or vocation.

This allowance may also be claimed by a married man whose wife is totally incapacitated (physically or mentally) throughout the year.

---

13   Can I claim tax relief on my life assurance premiums?

At one time tax relief for premiums paid on life assurance policies was allowed either as a coding allowance or as a deduction from the tax due shown on your assessment. Starting from the tax year 1979/80 the relief is given as a deduction by the payer from the premiums he pays, with certain restrictions. Known as "premium relief by deduction" the tax relief is therefore given without intervention by the tax office. The current deduction is 15%.

✸14   How can I prepare for my retirement?

During your working life you will pay national insurance contributions under a particular class (depending on whether you are an employee or self-employed), in the amounts laid down by the state. (See question 15 for more details regarding the various classes and amounts to be paid.) If you pay the full contributions for at least nine-tenths of your working life you will qualify for the full *basic retirement pension*. A woman entitled to a pension in her own right will normally receive it at the age of 60; a man at the age of 65. A married man will receive an additional amount for his wife but if she is entitled to pensions in respect of both her own and her husband's contributions, she may claim whichever is the higher pension.

In addition to paying national insurance contributions, if you are an employee you will also be paying into a pension scheme. There is a *national earnings-related pension scheme* run by the state, and since 1978 every employer has had to pay into the state scheme for all his employees unless he is running an *approved* private scheme in which case he can *contract out*.

If your employer has contracted out this will not affect your entitlement to the basic national insurance retirement pension or any other social security benefits.

Your employer may be running his scheme in-house or through a life assurance company, but irrespective of who is running the scheme, it *must be approved by the Inland Revenue Superannuation Funds Office* and by the *Occupational Pensions Board*. The benefits the scheme offers must be at least as good as those provided by the state scheme.

If the scheme is not approved by the Inland Revenue there can be various problems both for your employer and for yourself the employee, but this situation is very unlikely to arise in practice.

The state scheme offers a considerable improvement on the terms of pension schemes that were being run before 1978, and all the benefits increase in line with the increases in the Retail Price Index, but there are still a number of disadvantages that the state scheme has over an occupational scheme that has been duly approved. There can be no flexibility on the age of retirement, or a tax-free lump sum paid at retirement; there is no income tax relief for the individual's payments into the scheme, and at the present time (1982/83) earnings over £11,440 are unpensionable.

To a large extent these problems can be overcome by entering into an individual pension arrangement with an insurance company called a *top hat scheme*. If you have unpensioned salary (i.e. the amount in excess of £11,440) the arrangement can be made for just the excess; it is also possible to build into such arrangements benefits missing from the state scheme, such as tax-free lump sums on retirement, death in service benefits and to a certain extent it can be inflation proofed.

Finally if your employer pays the contribution it is not, in this instance, classed as a benefit and you will not have to pay tax on that amount; on the other hand you can obtain tax relief on your contributions provided they do not exceed 15% of your earnings.

If you are self-employed you may wish to prepare for your retirement by taking out a *retirement annuity policy* (see question 45). *This also applies to people who are in non-pensionable employment* (i.e. those not in a company scheme). There is a considerable range of self-employed pension schemes available, and the tax relief on the premiums must not be forgotten.

There are also avenues open to you such as *purchased life annuities*. This is where an individual invests some of his capital in an annuity; when he receives the annuity payments at a later date, part of the payment is treated as the return of his capital, and is not taxed; the remainder is taxed as unearned income. The split between capital and income will depend on the individual's age at the date of purchase of the annuity. There is *no tax relief on the cost of buying the annuity*. It is also possible for an individual aged over 65 to borrow on the security of his house, and provided that at least 90% of the loan is used to buy an annuity for himself (or him and his wife jointly) he can obtain tax relief on the loan interest paid (see question 19).

Another way of planning for your retirement is by careful investment of your capital in the years preceding that event, and there are various forms of investment to be considered (see question 21). Savings through life assurance can perhaps be bettered elsewhere, but life assurance should always be considered for protection purposes.

What national insurance contributions should I pay? 15 ✱

Although not strictly income tax, national insurance contributions are none the less a major cost to virtually all taxpayers. The Department of Health and Social Security publishes many leaflets giving guidance on national insurance matters to people in varying circumstances to help them determine the amount of contributions they should pay. This book does not attempt to cover every eventuality, but sets out below the classes of contributions and a few of the more common problems (the details shown are for 1982/83):

Class 1: Payable by all employees whose earnings are £29.50 or more per week (£127.83 a month, £1,534 a year) to a maximum of £220 per week (£953 a month, £11,440 a year). Deductions are made from the weekly or monthly salary by the employer (who also pays a contribution), using tables issued by the DHSS telling him the amount to deduct. The contributions vary depending on whether the employer is contracted in or contracted out – if it is the latter the contributions are lower as there is no payment to the state pension scheme.

Class 2: Payable by all self-employed people aged 16 to 65 (or 60 for women). Flat rate contribution of £3.75 per week: see 4 below.

Class 3: Voluntary flat rate contribution of £3.65 per week – paid by people wishing to improve their class 1 or 2 contribution record for the year to help them in qualifying for a limited range of benefits.

Class 4: Payable by the self-employed at 6% of net profits between £3,450 and £11,000 a year. Collected by way of the tax assessment issued by the Inland Revenue.

Other points to note:

1 If you are a *married woman* you may have chosen to pay reduced contributions under Class 1 – if so you must present your employer with a *certificate of reduced liabil-*

ity. This arrangement has now been closed and no new certificates are being issued.

2 If you are an *employee* you do not have to pay Class 1 contributions if you work after the age of 65 (60 for women) – you must then present your employer with a *certificate of age exemption* to prevent him from making the deductions.

3 If you have *more than one job* you may pay excessive contributions during the tax year – it is possible to claim a refund and there are leaflets explaining the procedure to follow.

4 If you are self-employed you may apply for *small earnings exemption from Class 2* contributions if you expect your earnings from self-employment to be less than a certain level (£1,600 in 1982/83).

5 If you are an *employee* and you are also *self-employed* you will be liable to pay Class 1 *and* Class 2 contributions (and possibly Class 4). Any excess paid will generally be refunded. *Payment of Class 2 and Class 4 contributions may be deferred* until after the end of the tax year and this avoids the need for a refund.

Remember – there are leaflets published by the Department of Health and Social Security which explain all of these situations (and many others) in full.

✳16   If I am over 65 years of age do I still pay tax?

Unfortunately, the United Kingdom tax system is not run in such a way as to automatically exempt you from tax when you reach the age of 65. If you are able to continue working after the normal retirement age, you will continue to pay tax on your income, and if you are receiving a pension, this too is taxable.

There is however an allowance which will be granted, if you are 65 or over in a year of assessment and your income falls within certain limits. In the case of a married couple it can be either the husband *or* the wife who is 65 or over to qualify for the relief. (If there is a wife's earnings election in force, the relief is calculated as for single claimants – see question 10.)

If your total income exceeds the stated limit, the allowance is reduced by two-thirds of the excess, until the allowance is reduced to the amount of the ordinary single or married personal allowance.

This relief may be index-linked in the same way as the other main personal allowances. For 1982/83 the reliefs and income limit are as follows:

	£
Single person's age allowance	2,070
Married person's age allowance	3,295
Income limit (irrespective of whether claimant is single or married)	6,700

Are all Social Security benefits taxable? 17

There are approximately 40 different benefits which are payable by the Department of Health and Social Security *none of which are taxable;* these include maternity benefit and grants, invalidity pensions, student grants, family income supplement, child benefit, sickness benefit and (from 6th April 1982) mobility allowance. **The following benefits are all taxable as earned income:**
Industrial death benefit
Invalid care allowance
Invalidity allowance when paid with retirement pension
Old person's pension
Retirement pension
War orphan's pension
Widowed mother's allowance
Widow's allowance
Widow's pension

Unemployment benefit (with effect from 6th July 1982)
Certain privately-operated sickness scheme benefits
(with effect from 6th April 1983)

✱18   What income tax reliefs can I claim in respect of my home?

If you do not own your own home you cannot claim any
allowance for the rent you pay. If you are buying your
own home for which you have taken out a mortgage with
a building society, you may have decided to take advantage of the special reduced rates of interest payable under
the *Mortgage Option Scheme* in which case *no tax relief is
available*. If this is not the case you may have taken out a
loan and wish to claim tax relief on the interest paid each
year, thus reducing the amount of your taxable income.

Loans for the purchase, improvement or development
of land, including buildings, are specifically allowable
for tax purposes, providing certain conditions are met.

At the time the interest is paid the property must be
the sole or main residence of the borrower, a dependent
relative of the borrower (or his/her spouse) living there
rent free, or a separated spouse. The loan *must* be used
for the purposes of purchasing or improving the house,
and not just by way of borrowing capital using the house
as security. The relief is limited to the first £25,000 of the
loan. Also allowable for income tax purposes is a bridg-
ing loan taken out for the purchase of one residence with
a view to the previous residence being sold; again the
relief is limited to the first £25,000 of the loan.

It should be emphasised that in any case tax relief can
only be claimed on the interest element of mortgage
payments and not on capital repayments.

You cannot normally claim for the day-to-day running
of your home but if you use part of your home as an office
you may be able to claim a tax allowance in respect of
lighting and heating etc. The Revenue is sometimes

reluctant to allow such claims, taking the view that if an employer requires you to do "paperwork" he will provide you with an office. However, claims are accepted if you can prove it is *necessary* to work at home, whether you are an employee or self-employed. *Beware* however of making a claim that you use part of your home *exclusively* for these purposes as you may find the exemption from capital gains tax on your own home is affected (see question 72).

At present, mortgage interest is paid "gross", i.e. without any deduction, and relief is given in the PAYE coding or through the assessment. With effect from 6th April 1983, relief will be given by deduction, so that the taxpayer will deduct tax at the basic rate from the interest payments and pay only the "net" amount to the lenders. The administrative arrangements for this change are still being looked at by the Revenue and borrowers will be advised as to what action to take in due course.

What other loan interest can I claim?　19

The rules regarding relief for other loan interest are very strict and relief will not be granted unless the loan proceeds are applied for the qualifying purpose within a reasonable length of time. Similarly, if the loan is used for some other purpose first, the relief will not be granted. There is no tax relief for overdraft interest or credit cards (or similar arrangements), unless it is incurred wholly and exclusively for the purposes of your business as a sole trader or partner and is charged directly in your business accounts.

Loan interest relief will be allowed if the proceeds of the loan are used for any of the following, all of which are *qualifying purposes:*

1 A loan in respect of property which is let at a commer-

cial rent for at least 26 weeks of the year and when not being let, is available to be let or undergoing repair. (There may be some restrictions as to the relief available.)

2 Provision is also made to cover the situation where the borrower is living in accommodation provided by the employer as one of the requirements of his job, but at the same time the employee is paying interest on a loan to buy a house which he is either using as a residence at the time or intends to so use within 12 months; this allows relief to be claimed for interest paid by the employee on a loan on a house bought in anticipation of moving out of his present "job related" living accommodation. (Relief on maximum £25,000 loan only.)

3 A loan for purchase of plant or machinery for use in a trade if the borrower is a partner in the business, or for use in the borrower's office or employment. Relief is only granted for three years, and only if a claim for capital allowances on the plant and machinery has been granted.

4 A loan for purchase of ordinary shares in, or making a loan to a close company, subject to certain restrictions.

5 A loan for purchase of a share of, or making a loan to, a partnership. The lender must be a member of the partnership; where the money is lent to the partnership it must be used for the purposes of the partnership business.

6 A loan to make payment of capital transfer tax or estate duty in respect of a deceased person. The relief is granted to the personal representatives, but for a period of one year only from the date of the loan.

7 A loan to purchase a life annuity by a borrower aged 65 or over. He must use his own home as security for the loan and at least 90% of the proceeds of the loan must be used to purchase the annuity (see question 14).

Relief was also available up to 5th April 1982 on loans taken out before 27th March 1974 which did not qualify for relief under any of the above provisions.

Remember you may claim loan interest in respect of a loan taken out to purchase or improve your home (see question 18).

Do I pay tax on my bank interest? 20

Bank interest is *not taxed before you receive it* and it is therefore taxable in the hands of the recipient. The normal basis of assessment is "preceding year", i.e. whatever is credited to your bank account in one tax year is taxed in the following tax year. There are special rules for the interest credited during the opening and closing years of a bank account when the interest may be taxed in the same year it is credited to the account.

Interest credited to the National Savings Bank *ordinary* account is exempt up to £70 a year for an individual. If you are married, each spouse will be entitled to the £70 exemption but any excess of one spouse's exemption *cannot* be given to the other. Any interest in excess of £70 is taxed in the usual way. NB: the exemption does *not* apply to the National Savings Bank *investment account*.

Where should I invest my capital? 21

This is a topic which could be the subject matter of a book in its own right. There is no one answer because matters such as the availability of your capital (i.e. the need to have quick access to capital), provision for your dependents, how much you want to invest and your own personal tax position must be taken into consideration. It is therefore not possible to list different forms of investment and to advise on which ones to use without knowing about your overall financial position – this is something for you to discuss with your professional advisers. What follows therefore are a few *general* words of advice.

There are certain types of investment on which you *do not* pay tax; these include the *National Savings Bank* ordinary account (see question 20) where up to £70 interest can be credited to your account without tax being payable. There are also *National Savings Certificates,* on which interest, bonuses and any other sums are exempt from all forms of tax; there is a limit to the number of these you may hold. There is also a special index linked issue (previously known as "granny bonds"). You may wish to invest in *Premium Bonds* – if you do so, remember there is no interest on the amount invested but if you should win, your winnings are not taxable.

Many people invest their capital in *building societies* – indeed very often this is a necessity if you are hoping to obtain a mortgage – and the interest you receive is net of tax. A point to note arises here: if you are not liable to pay tax at all, investing your money in a building society is *not* a good idea, as you are deemed to have paid tax on the interest but this cannot be reclaimed.

The rate of interest on ordinary share accounts is quite reasonable but if you do not require immediate access to your capital a *Save As You Earn Scheme* is always a good investment. Building societies have SAYE schemes and there is also a National Savings SAYE scheme run by the Department of National Savings. Such an investment is one of the best ways to earn a high rate of interest, but it is a longer term commitment to saving, as you will be required to pay a fixed sum every month for a period of up to five years. The National Savings scheme is linked to the Retail Price Index and therefore keeps pace with inflation: whatever you receive back is tax-free. *Beware* of stopping the payments early as penalties can be incurred. It is possible to invest in both the National Savings scheme *and* a building society scheme, if you so wish.

Whatever the amount of capital you wish to invest you will obviously require a certain amount that is realisable to provide cash in an emergency (the alternatives mentioned above, with the exception of the SAYE schemes, might be best in this respect) but you may wish to consider investing in *Government gilt-edged stocks*. The income you receive from these investments is taxed at source (at the basic rate of tax) and if you hold the securities for longer than 12 months there is no liability to capital gains tax (see question 68).

Following the 1982 Budget, the special issues of inflation linked gilt-edged stocks which were previously only available to pension funds and similar bodies are now being made available to all categories of investor. These provide a measure of tax-free capital appreciation which could be attractive to higher rate tax payers.

Another worthwhile form of investment is the *single premium investment bond*. A capital sum is invested with an insurance company; the income is taxable but you are allowed to withdraw each year up to 5% of the initial value invested and these withdrawals are not immediately taxed. They are taken into account in the year the bond is surrendered, and both higher rate tax and investment income surcharge are payable in this final year. It is possible however to reduce this liability with careful planning, and making sure that the year of encashment is one when other income is low.

If you are already a higher-rate tax payer you should be seeking to minimise your tax liability, possibly by aiming for capital growth. This may result in your having to resort from time to time to capital, to supplement your income, unless you also have other forms of investment.

If you are considering investing directly on the stock market, for many people unit trusts represent the most sensible and effective way of doing so. The clearing banks and Trustee Savings Banks offer a wide range of savings schemes which could also be considered.

With an uncertain future with regard to inflation, it is wise to have a *flexible investment policy* rather than allow yourself to become too restricted. It might well be prudent, therefore, even if your aim is for a higher income, to invest some of your funds in investments producing lower income than perhaps could be obtained otherwise, in order to achieve *flexibility*, the *security* of your capital, and the prospects of *capital growth* – all to try and beat inflation.

✱22 Can a deed of covenant save me tax?

Deeds of covenant do not provide spectacular tax savings, but they are nevertheless useful weapons for you to have. They can be very simple to create and easy to operate. They do not involve a commitment for too long a period and they can provide useful savings in a variety of situations.

A deed of covenant is the "gratuitous transfer" by one person (the "covenantor") of some part of his income to another person (the "beneficiary"). Below are two of the main provisions which limit the use of deeds of covenent in tax planning:

1 If the income is given for a period not exceeding six years "it is not recognised for tax purposes" – hence the familiar seven-year covenant.

2 The transfer of income by a parent to a child under 18 and unmarried has no effect for tax purposes as this income is still deemed to be that of the parent. The covenant can still be effective, however, if it is made by a grandparent or other relative.

The "seven-year" rule calls for a little ingenuity – the period covered by the deed of covenant must be able to *exceed* six years to qualify for tax purposes – it is no good making the payment "for six years" as this clearly cannot exceed the limit. Thus, the deed of covenant must either be of a *definite duration exceeding six years* or of *an indefinite duration,* which is *capable of exceeding six years.* Examples of this are the lifetime of the covenantor or the beneficiary or, if the covenant is in respect of a child, until the beneficiary *ceases in full-time education.* At first glance, if the beneficiary is taking only a three year course this would not seem to qualify, but if the beneficiary was to fail exams etc. it may be that his educational time is extended – in other words, the period is capable of exceeding six years.

On the other hand, if the duration of the covenant was for the lifetime of the covenantor and he (unfortunately) died after four years, the "duration" test is still fulfilled. At the time the covenant was made the duration of the covenant was for an indefinite period (i.e. the lifetime of the covenantor) which was *capable* of exceeding six years.

Deeds of covenant in respect of children over 18 attending university are popular, which is why the above illustration concerning the duration of the covenant has been used. The abolition of tax allowances for children has greatly increased the usefulness of deeds of covenant, particularly *where the child is a student at university and the parent is expected, under the grant regulations, to make a contribution to the student's maintenance.*

Parents are not asked to make a contribution if their income is insufficient, so if you are asked to contribute, your income must be high enough to warrant you paying at least the basic rate tax. *For the covenant to be effective you must be paying tax on at least the same amount of your income, as the amount of the covenant.* In other words, tax on the amount you are to pay has already been deducted from you (albeit on your other income). If you make a covenant in respect of your child (possibly equal to the amount of the parental contribution for the first year) *you will only have to pay the net amount* to your son or daughter: in other words tax is deducted before the student receives it and you have saved the tax on the payment. It is advisable to keep the amount of the covenant to within the single personal allowance (which the child is entitled to) as *he can then reclaim the tax that was deducted*, by making a claim to the Inland Revenue, and he will then have received the gross "parental" contribution.

Example

Ivor Sunn's eldest boy Jack is at university and his father is required to contribute £700 per annum towards his maintenance. He therefore enters into a deed of covenant for an annual amount which after deduction of income tax at the basic rate for the time being will leave £700, for a period of seven years, the lifetimes of the covenantor or beneficiary, or the period during which the beneficiary is undergoing full-time education or training. Jack has no other taxable income in the year 1982/83.

The net cost to the father is the amount he actually pays, i.e. £700 per year. Jack is treated as receiving income of £1,000 gross less income tax at 30% of £300; because his taxable income is less than the single personal allowance for the year (£1,565) he is not liable to income tax in 1982/83 and can therefore reclaim the £300 treated as deducted, from the Inland Revenue, giving him a total actual income of £1,000.

In order to substantiate the claim it is essential that the amount provided in the deed of covenant is actually paid over to the beneficiary.

A similar arrangement applies to covenanted payments to *charities;* as charities are exempt from tax they are able to recover from the Inland Revenue the income tax treated as deducted from the payments made by the donor at no extra cost to the latter, thus providing a substantial boost to their own revenue.

Recent legislation has brought in two changes of particular importance to the making of covenanted payments to charities:

1 For the year 1980/81 and thereafter, a deed of covenant to a charity need only run for a period "capable of exceeding *three* years" instead of six, as the general rule requires; this it is hoped will encourage people to commit themselves for four years when they might have been reluctant to go on for seven years.

2 For the tax year 1981/82 and thereafter, a covenantor is able to obtain relief for higher rate tax purposes (including the investment income surcharge, see question 2) for such payments made to charities. It should be emphasised that the charity can still only recover the basic rate element of tax, but the real cost to the donor will be reduced by the further tax relief he can claim if he is paying income tax at more than the basic rate. There is an upper limit of £3,000 gross a year to this relief.

Example

Charitable covenant (taxpayer paying top rate of 75%)		£70 net p.a.
Income tax, recoverable by charity		£30
		£100
Gross equivalent		£100
Income tax relief due to covenantor by deemed deduction at 30%	£30	
by relief at (75 − 30)%	£45	
		£75
Net cost to donor		£25

NB: the final point: A deed of covenant is a formal legal document and must be properly drawn up to have the required effect. Most charities use standard forms which have been approved by the Inland Revenue for this purpose; in other cases it is *essential* to obtain proper professional advice on the drafting of a deed of covenant to ensure that it works.

---

23   Can I set aside money towards my taxes?

It is possible to set money aside to pay your taxes by way of *certificates of tax deposit*. Some people prefer this method of payment of tax to having to withdraw money from another source to pay their tax bill. The deposits are made with the Collector of Taxes for the subsequent payment of tax generally (except for PAYE and tax deducted from subcontractors in the construction industry). The minimum initial deposit is £2,000 with minimum additions of £500. Interest is payable gross, but is taxable, and this will accrue for a maximum of six years from the date of deposit to the date the tax is due to be paid. If a deposit is withdrawn for cash at any time, a reduced rate of interest will apply.

---

24   I have other sources of income which are not taxed at source: how are they taxed?

Two of the most common types of income you may receive which are not taxed at source (and which are not dealt with elsewhere) are income from furnished lettings and property. These are dealt with as follows:
Furnished lettings: An assessment is made on the profits arising in the year, which is rent received less rent

paid, repairs, rates, commission and any other expenses relating to the letting. There are also allowances to be claimed for wear and tear of the furniture. If you provide a service, i.e. cleaning, laundry, etc., the lettings may amount to a trade and be taxed as earnings from self-employment.

Income from property: Tax is charged on rents received from property including rents from leases of land and buildings, ground rents, feu duties etc. The assessments are made on the basis of receipts arising in the year of assessment, less allowable deductions such as repairs, rates, electricity etc., insurance premiums, valuation fees, costs of rent collection.

For both these types of income – make sure you claim all the expenses to keep the taxable amount to a minimum.

If I have income subject to overseas taxation can I get any relief in the United Kingdom? 25

The United Kingdom tax system is such that it taxes income if it arises in this country, or income wherever it arises, if the person entitled to receive it is resident here. If you are entitled to receive income from overseas, due to the fact that other countries have similar wide powers of taxation, it is inevitable that some income will be taxed twice. It is impossible to avoid this unless there is one universal tax system, but in many cases where income suffers tax in two countries it is possible to claim *double taxation relief*.

There are double taxation treaties between the United Kingdom and some 90 other countries and in general, either a particular source of income is exempt from tax in one of the countries involved, or the relief for foreign direct taxation is given as a credit against the corresponding United Kingdom tax.

This is a complex area and special consideration needs to be given to each situation.

✹ 26   What happens when I die?

When you die, if there is outstanding income tax to pay this liability will have to be met by your personal representatives. The implications of capital gains tax and capital transfer tax are dealt with elsewhere.

If you are married the tax position depends on which of the spouses dies first. If the wife dies first, the husband will still be entitled to claim the married man's personal allowance for the whole of the tax year, and from the start of the next tax year he will be taxed as a single person. It is possible for the husband (or his executors) to disclaim responsibility for the wife's tax outstanding at her death, providing due notice is given to the Inland Revenue, normally within two months of the grant of probate.

If it is the husband who dies first, the wife's income from the beginning of the tax year to the date of his death is included in his final assessment to tax. She is then treated as a single person for the remainder of that tax year and subsequent years, being given the lower personal allowance (see question 5) against her income which presumably will include a widow's pension. In addition, recent legislation has introduced a *widow's bereavement allowance* to be claimed by the widow for the year in which her husband dies. The relief is available against her income following his death and is equivalent to the difference between the single and married man's personal allowances (i.e. for 1982/83 £880). The allowance may be claimed if the husband was "entitled" to the married person's allowance, even if the allowance had actually been foregone due to a wife's earnings election being in force.

II
You've Earned It
TAXATION OF THE EMPLOYEE

27   What is included in my earnings for income tax purposes and how are they taxed under the PAYE system?

Earnings from an office or employment come under many different names such as salaries, wages, fees, overtime, bonuses, commission, tips and gratuities etc. *In general, anything which you receive as a reward for your services is taxable,* and the words "emoluments" and "remuneration" are often used to cover all receipts of this nature.

Having decided what is taxable, the next problem is how is it taxed? As an employee, you are probably only too well aware of the tax that is deducted from the pay you receive each week or month under the *Pay As You Earn* (PAYE) scheme.

The PAYE system was introduced in 1943 to replace other less successful methods of taxing the earnings of employees. It was not introduced as a new method of assessment; it was, and still is, merely a *scheme for the collection of tax*. Its aim is to deduct tax from each payment of remuneration, the deduction rising and falling as the pay rises and falls, so that at the end of the income tax year, the tax deducted during the year is sufficient having regard to the employee's personal circumstances and no further action is necessary.

The backbone of the system is the *cumulative* principle under which, as the tax year progresses, running (cumulative) totals are kept of the amounts of remuneration received from the beginning of the tax year and of the tax deducted. Each time your employer pays remuneration he will deduct (or refund) an amount of tax which will keep the total figure deducted correct. He can tell what this figure should be from tax tables which are supplied by the Inland Revenue. The process continues up to week 52 or month 12, when a new income tax year starts, and you commence at week 1 or month 1 again.

You already know that the amount of tax payable is governed by your personal circumstances and there are certain reliefs and allowances you may claim. If the employer is to deduct the right amount of tax it would seem that he too must have knowledge of your personal circumstances but the Revenue are bound not to reveal to anyone the private information given to them. The difficulty is resolved by the use of *codes*, with a number and a letter from which the employer can only tell certain things (i.e. in most cases he can tell if you are a single or married man, but if you do not wish him to know this, it can be prevented). The allowances to which you are entitled are added together and the code number resulting from this is notified to the employer – *the higher the code number, the lower the tax*. Your employer will only be informed of the final code but you will be sent a notice showing all your coding allowances; if you disagree with the code you may appeal against it. Similarly, if your personal circumstances change during the year the Revenue should be notified and your code will be amended. Because of the cumulative principle mentioned above, a change of code has retrospective effect to the previous 6th April. If it is increased, the tax over-deducted in previous weeks or months is refunded by your employer. If it is decreased, a special basis called Week 1 or Month 1 is used, otherwise the tax underdeducted in the previous weeks would be deductible in one sum, and this could cause hardship. In effect, in this situation the cumulative principle is abandoned for that year, and the employer deducts tax on each pay day without reference to previous pay. (See question 28 for what happens to the tax underdeducted for the early part of the year.)

The previous paragraphs may give the impression that employees stay with one employer all the time but of course people change their jobs, school leavers start work for the first time, elderly people retire and in fact there is a constant movement. To prevent the entire PAYE system breaking down, when you leave one employer he will give you a form P45 showing your code number and pay and tax to date; this you must give to your new employer to enable him to continue the cumulative deductions of tax. If you lose your P45, or for some other reason are starting work without it, your employer will use a special code so that your tax does not fall too far into arrears, and will inform the Revenue so that they may start the procedure for issuing the correct code.

With effect from 6th July 1982, unemployment benefit is to be taxable as earned income (see question 17). The actual benefit payments will be made without deduction of tax to benefit claimants, but these will be taken into account in determining whether any part of the tax deducted under PAYE prior to the period of unemployment is to be refunded. Any refund will be made only when the individual starts work again or at the end of the tax year, whichever is the sooner.

---

28   If I pay tax under PAYE will I also be assessed at the end of each year? If so, how will I be assessed?

It has already been explained that the PAYE system is not a method of assessment but simply a way of collecting the tax. The next point to consider is how much of the earnings are assessed for a particular year. *The proper basis of assessment is to assess the amount actually earned in the year of assessment.* Most employees receive at the end of each week or month the amount of money they have actually earned during that period. If at the end of the tax year they are therefore assessed on what they have earned, this is the same figure as the amount they have received and tax has already been deducted. The employer sends to the Revenue details of each person's pay and tax deducted, on what is called a *deduction card* – the details are checked and if the tax deducted is correct, no further action is normally required.

If you ask for an assessment because you think you have paid the wrong amount of tax the Revenue will do as you ask, but the Revenue also has the right to make an assessment where it is considered necessary. This includes situations where there is tax owing for an earlier year, or where an allowance has been given incorrectly. Any refund of tax due to you resulting from the assessment is repaid to you, but if there is an underpayment of tax this will be collected from you.

This is normally achieved by restricting your coding allowances for the following year, although there are occasions when you will be asked to make payment of the tax direct to the Collector of Taxes. (You may voluntarily pay the tax to the Collector if you prefer this method of payment to having your coding allowances restricted.) Also collected through a later code number are underpayments arising because an allowance was removed from the code part way through a year and there is tax to pay for the period before the code was amended. If, in any of these instances, to collect the tax in one year would cause hardship this may be spread over a period of up to three years. No action is taken to collect small amounts and a particularly lenient view is normally taken with regard to pensioners.

Cases like these do not normally present any real problem but in situations where there are *substantial*

fluctuations in remuneration (e.g. fees, bonuses, commission etc), the basis of assessment is more complicated as
the payment of the remuneration is often made in a
different tax year to when it was actually earned. *The
assessment must exclude any payments made during the year
which relate to a previous year, and include payments relating to the year in question but which will not be paid until
after the end of the tax year.* This is called the "earnings"
basis of assessment and the business accounts of the
employer must be consulted to see what commissions
etc. have been voted during the tax year so that the
assessment is correct, although payment may not be
made to the individual until a later date. Any payments
which relate to more than one tax year are apportioned to
arrive at the actual amount *earned* in each year.

As part of the information necessary to raise an
assessment is taken from the employer's business
accounts, there may be some delay before the details are
available and the assessment is therefore also delayed: to
prevent some of this delay there is an alternative basis of
assessment, which, although it has no legal foundation,
may nevertheless be acceptable both to the Inland
Revenue and yourself. On this basis the assessment is
made on the figure of remuneration shown in the employer's accounts for their accounting year that ends in the
year of assessment (this is known as the "accounts" basis
of assessment). This avoids the necessity of apportioning
the income for the accounting year over two income tax
years. The method of strict apportionment is always
used when the income first arises and ceases. The
Revenue will not use the "accounts" basis unless they
have your written agreement. (If you have a problem as
to how your remuneration is to be assessed, you should
seek professional advice.)

Although the figure of remuneration shown in an
employer's records at the end of the tax year is not always
used in an assessment, the figure of tax deducted is

always used. It may well be that because of this a large underpayment of tax is produced, but in most cases this will be carried forward to the later year when the payment is made of remuneration that has already been assessed, and the tax paid at the time will cover the underpayment; the Revenue will not normally seek to collect tax from you on remuneration you have not yet received.

How much can I receive tax free when I cease my employment? 29

First of all, one very important point must be made – if you have a contract of employment which provides for a termination payment, such a sum is taxable in full. However, it is understood that a payment in lieu of notice is not taxable even if it is made under a clause in the contract, because this option is in any case open to an employer under the employment legislation.

In other cases there have been recent changes. Prior to 6th April 1981, there was normally a tax-free limit for termination payments of £10,000 with complex rules as to the calculation of tax on the excess. For the year ended 5th April 1982, the tax-free limit was raised to £25,000 with tax on the excess being reduced by half the tax that would normally be payable.

From 6th April 1982, the rules have again been changed. The tax-free limit remains at £25,000; on the next £25,000, the tax payable is reduced by a half, and on the £25,000 above that by a quarter. Any excess over £75,000 remains taxable in full.

It is important that termination payments are correctly identified and that references to them in correspondence, minutes of board meetings etc. are worded in a way that does not suggest that they are payments for past or present services as they would then be charged to tax as income from that employment.

To obtain the maximum benefit for this relief it is helpful to keep other income as low as possible in the year in which the payment is taxable, so if a new employment is to be taken up immediately, termination should be as near to the end of the tax year as possible, to avoid increasing other income.

Statutory redundancy payments are exempt from tax but may still be taken into account in these calculations.

30 Are perks taxable?

Most employees like a job that has perks and many employers nowadays run some form of incentive scheme or give their employees a benefit of some description. Unfortunately, the majority of these *fringe benefits*, as they are called, are taxable, although in some cases this depends on whether you are a higher paid employee with earnings in excess of £8,500, or a director (in which case the level of your remuneration is irrelevant). Because of the method of taxing fringe benefits it is nearly always to your advantage to be given an item as a benefit instead of having to buy the same item out of your own net income which has already suffered tax. It is not possible to list in this book all the possible benefits your employer may consider, but in the following table are mentioned some of the more popular choices:

Benefit	*Directors and employees earning over £8,500 per annum*	*Employees earning less than £8,500 per annum*
Holidays	Taxable in full unless combined with a business trip, when the "holiday element" may still be taxable	Not taxable providing employer pays direct and does not reimburse employee

Season tickets	Taxable	Taxable from 1982/83 onwards
Suggestion scheme payments	Not taxable provided it is reasonable and not a term of contract	As aside.
Prize incentive schemes	Taxable	Taxable
Examination prizes	Not taxable (as for suggestion schemes)	As aside
Canteen facilities	Not taxable provided available in one form or another to all staff	Not taxable
Luncheon vouchers	Not taxable providing not in excess of 15p per day	As aside
Credit cards	Taxable	Taxable from 1982/83 onwards
Medical insurance premium	Taxable	Taxable up to and including 1981/82; not taxable thereafter

The special rules relating to company cars (still far and away the most popular perk) are dealt with in question 31.

If a company should transfer any of its assets to an employee, such as living accommodation, a motor car, etc., the employee will be taxable on the market value of the asset at the time of its transfer. There are also special rules if an employee has living accommodation provided by his employer.

As has already been stated this is only a brief outline of the taxation of some of the fringe benefits: if you wish to know more about these matters you should seek professional advice.

---

31 What is my tax position if I have a company car, or use my own car for business purposes?

If you are provided with a company car and you use it for your own private purposes, you are obviously deriving a benefit from this, simply due to the fact you are using a car that does not belong to you for your own private use. On the other hand, if you are using your own car for business purposes this must benefit your employer and if he does not reimburse the expenses you incur, you would be out of pocket. This is, in simple terms, the way you and your car are considered for tax purposes.

If you are a director or an employee earning over £8,500 per annum and you have a company car, you are taxed on what the Revenue consider is the benefit you receive from using the car for your own use. This is often referred to as the "table benefit" because the benefit is decided according to the age, cost and cylinder capacity of the car, worked out according to tables included in the legislation. For the current year, if your business mileage exceeds 18,000 the benefit is *reduced to one half*. Also, if your business mileage is less than 2,500 miles a year this is classed as insubstantial and the benefit is $1\frac{1}{2}$ times the normal figure. If you use your own car for business purposes you may claim a tax allowance as if you are self-employed (see question 43) but when the allowance has been computed any amount received from your employer as reimbursement is deducted.

With effect from 6th April 1982, petrol provided by an employer for the private use of a director or employee earning over £8,500 per annum is to be taxed; previously under certain circumstances this escaped any charge.

In any event *no allowance* is given for *travelling from home to work* as this is not classed as business mileage. The rule is that expenses must be incurred *wholly, exclusively and necessarily* in "the performance of the duties of the employment" to be allowable and this does not cover travelling expenses *to* that place of employment.

**I have always lived in this country but part of my work is now   32
done abroad: can I claim any tax relief?**

You are now entering into the complicated areas of domicile and residence and it is important you have a basic understanding of these terms before the reliefs available for work done abroad are explained. However what follows in this section is very simplified and some matters are mentioned only briefly. If you intend leaving this country to work abroad, either temporarily or permanently, it is recommended you refer to *Working Abroad*, The Daily Telegraph guide to working and living overseas. In this 312-page book Godfrey Golzen and Margaret Stewart tell you how to get a job overseas, what salary to expect, what to do about your children's education and how your UK tax and NHS status will be affected (£5.50 by post from Department X, The Daily Telegraph, 135 Fleet Street, London EC4).

Generally, your *domicile* is the country you think of as your natural homeland, which is normally that of your origin at birth. It is possible to change your domicile to one of your choice, but only if you sever all connections with the country of your origin and produce evidence of your intention to settle permanently in the other country.

Once it is known in what country you are domiciled, your *residence status* has to be decided for a tax year as this can decide how much of your earnings are taxed for that year, as you will see later. There are three phrases involved here – resident, ordinarily resident and not resident. *Resident* and *not resident* are factual terms meaning, as you would expect, that you are either living in this country at the time or you are not. The term *ordinarily resident* refers to someone who normally lives in this country, although he may be abroad at the present time. A wife's residence status is independent of that of her husband; if their status should differ for a tax year, husband and wife are treated as separate individuals unless it is to their disadvantage.

The following reliefs apply to someone who is *domiciled, resident and ordinarily resident* in the United Kingdom, and whose *employer* is also *resident* in this country.

1 Where the duties of an employment are performed wholly or partly outside the United Kingdom and the time spent abroad is at least 365 days, there is no United Kingdom tax on these earnings. There are provisions relaxing the 365 day requirement when time spent in this country does not exceed 62 consecutive days or 1/6th of the time elapsed since the first day of absence (this last rule can operate harshly towards the beginning of a lengthy absence period). The exemption is only available against the earnings in respect of work performed abroad (i.e. normally earnings in respect of work done in this country are fully taxable).

2 Where the duties of an employment are performed wholly or partly outside the United Kingdom and the time spent abroad in relation to that employment is at least *30 qualifying days* then 25% of the earnings relating to the duties performed overseas are exempt from United Kingdom tax. There are conditions to be fulfilled before a day spent abroad can be classed as a *qualifying day:* the employee must be absent from this country at the end of the day, and the day itself must either be substantially devoted to the performance of the duties of that employment overseas, or travelling in or for the

performance of those duties, or be one of seven consecutive days of absence from this country which taken together are again substantially devoted to the performance of the duties overseas.

Travelling expenses to take up or return from an overseas employment are not taxable; also tax free are board and lodging and expenses of travelling between different overseas employments. Costs of travel for wife and children may also be included under certain conditions.

If you are leaving the country to work abroad you are required to complete a questionnaire for the Revenue so that a ruling can be made as to your residence status. In the situations looked at so far the employer is resident in the United Kingdom so he will operate Pay As You Earn in the usual way (see question 27). Where it is clear that the 100% deduction will apply (1 above) a special code is issued so that the employer may pay the relevant remuneration without deducting tax. Where the 25% deduction is applicable (2 above) there may be an estimated amount allowed in the code number or in certain circumstances PAYE will only be operated on 75% of the relevant remuneration.

Where the 25% deduction applies to services performed partly abroad in this way, the amount of remuneration to which the deduction is applied is usually found on a strict time basis by applying the fraction:

$$\frac{\text{number of ``qualifying days''}}{365}$$

to the remuneration for the tax year.

Example

In the year 1982/83 Hastie spends 70 qualifying days on overseas work for his company. His salary for the year is £16,000.

	£
Actual remuneration	16,000
Less deduction	

$$\frac{16,000 \times 70 \times 25\%}{365}$$

	767
Amount assessable	15,233

There is provision for the taxpayer to claim a larger deduction than on the strict *pro rata* basis where the particular circumstances of the case may be thought to justify it but it is known that the Inland Revenue are very reluctant to move away from the strict basis set out above.

If you are working abroad for a time and are employed by an employer who is resident overseas, 25% of these earnings are exempt from United Kingdom tax; no test as to "qualifying days" abroad is required in this case. If foreign tax is suffered it may be possible to claim double taxation relief (see question 25).

Generally where the 25% or 100% deductions are claimed the Inland Revenue are likely to scrutinise the arrangements to ensure that the remuneration paid is reasonable in relation to the duties performed and in particular that there is no "loading" of remuneration against which a deduction is claimed as compared with that against which no deduction applies.

Now turning to the taxation of a *non-resident* the basic rule is that a non-resident's employment earnings are taxed in the United Kingdom only insofar as they are attributable to any duties of that employment which are performed in this country. In instances where duties are carried out partly in this country and partly overseas, separate contracts of employment are strongly recommended. If duties are normally performed overseas, any duties performed in this country will still be treated as if they were performed overseas provided they are merely *incidental* to the overseas duties. A decision obviously has to be made as to what is classified as "incidental": in general, it is not the time spent in this country which is the deciding factor, but if duties in this country occupy more than three months in a tax year, they cannot normally be said to be incidental. The Revenue will take into account the nature of the duties and their relationship to the overseas duties. (Again, remember that if any of the income is taxed in both countries it may be possible to claim double taxation relief – see question 25.) Personal reliefs for United Kingdom income tax are basically only available to a United Kingdom resident, but certain categories of non-residents can claim a proportion of them.

I have always lived abroad but now I have come to work in the United Kingdom: what is my tax position?   33

If you were born abroad and have always lived in that country your "domicile" will generally be your country of origin as explained in the previous question. If you are *not domiciled in the United Kingdom but are resident and ordinarily resident* in this country (i.e. you are living here for six months or more in a tax year and you habitually live in this country), the general rules as to paying income tax are as follows: any income arising within the United Kingdom is chargeable to tax in full, and income arising outside the United Kingdom is chargeable to tax only by reference to the amounts which are remitted to the UK.

If the *employer is resident abroad* and *you the employee are domiciled abroad* the earnings you receive from that employer are called *foreign emoluments* and your residence status affects the amount that is taxed. If you are *resident and ordinarily resident,* income tax is only charged on 50% of that amount. If you have been resident in the United Kingdom for at least nine out of the ten preceding years the relief is reduced to 25% (i.e. you will pay tax on 75% of your earnings). If you are *resident but not ordinarily resident* (i.e. you are living here for six months or more in a particular tax year but you do *not* live here normally) the relief is given against only the earnings received in respect of duties performed in this country. With regard to the duties performed overseas, United Kingdom tax will only be charged on any remittances that are sent to this country.

It should be made clear that these rules do not apply to individuals whose domicile is the Republic of Ireland and who are employed by an employer resident in the Republic; their earnings are specifically excluded from the definition of "foreign emoluments" so as not to qualify for the 50% or 25% relief.

A person who is resident in the United Kingdom may claim the personal allowances discussed in earlier questions.

34 Are there any other expenses I can claim?

It cannot be emphasised too often that expenses are only allowable if they are incurred wholly, exclusively and necessarily in the performance of the duties of your employment. There must therefore be no question of the expenses being partly for your own benefit and they must be absolutely necessary for you to carry out your duties. A great number of the claims made to the Revenue which fail, do so on the test of necessity.

You have already seen that the costs of travelling to work from home are generally not deductible because the costs are not incurred in the course of performing the duties, but in order to get to the place where the duties are to be performed. Travelling expenses *will* be allowed provided they were incurred necessarily in the performance of the duties of the office. It is generally accepted that travel expenses include the cost of accommodation while travelling.

You may wish to make a claim that part of your home is used as an office – this is covered in question 18. If, in addition to this, you purchase books etc., you may find it difficult to prove that they are wholly, necessarily and exclusively for the performance of your duties. If you pay subscriptions to a *recognised* body, such as a professional institute, the amount you pay is an allowable expense.

Similarly, if you are a manual worker there are fixed deductions agreed, depending on the actual nature of your employment and the industry in which you are employed.

Remember – expenses will only be allowed if they are incurred *wholly, exclusively and necessarily in the performance of your duties.*

III
Now You're in Business
TAXATION OF THE SELF-EMPLOYED

35   What happens when I start up in business?

Special rules apply for taxation purposes when a business first commences and when it ceases, otherwise tax would not be paid until a business was well under way, and would also be payable some time after it had ceased. Because of these rules tax savings are possible, if matters are timed correctly and the accounting date is chosen with care (see question 36).

It is important to determine the actual date on which a business commences as this also decides the first assessment for tax purposes. *The first year of assessment will tax the actual profits from the date the business started to the next 5th April* (i.e. end of the tax year). This will most probably mean the assessment is made on a proportion of the profits shown in the first accounts (computed on a time basis).

The second assessment will tax the profits of the first 12 months trading, from the date of commencement; however, if the first accounts are for a period of *less* than 12 months, the second and third years assessments will also be made on a time basis (which would most probably mean a proportion of the profit from the first two sets of accounts). If the *first accounts were prepared for a 12 month period* the third year's assessment will be based on the first accounts. This is called the *previous year basis of assessment* and will continue throughout the period of self-employment until the final years (i.e. the profits of your accounting period *ending* in the tax year 1982/83 will actually be *taxed* in 1983/84).

You do have an option that *all* the first three years of assessment be made on the actual profits for those years. This is only to be done if it is to your advantage (i.e. if the figures are smaller than those produced by the normal basis) and the election will normally only be made if the profits of the second and third accounting periods are lower than those earned in the first year of trading. Claims must be made within six years from the end of the third year of assessment.

If an election is not advantageous the first accounting period will be the basis for the first three years tax assessments, so it is important that the tax profits be kept as low as possible. If you consult your professional advisers they will ensure that this is achieved and that all allowances and expenses are claimed (including capital allowances and stock relief which are dealt with in questions 42 and 44).

How do I choose my accounting date? 36

Most people when left to their own devices will automatically prepare accounts for the first twelve months trading without seeking further advice: admittedly this has one advantage of enabling the first three years tax assessments to be issued, but that is all. Other people prepare accounts for the calendar year or even the tax year. You should always consult a professional adviser before you choose your accounting date as there may be an advantage in your choosing a particular date depending on the line of business you are in. As a general guide, the date that has the most advantages is one early in the tax year (e.g. 30th April). You must remember that the choice of your accounting date is not so much a way of saving tax, but of deferring payment of that tax, and this is brought about due to the preceding year basis of assessment mentioned in the previous question.

As you have seen, the basis of assessment means that the profits you make during one year will not be taxed until the following year. To illustrate the point, the examples below use two different accounting dates – 30th September and 30th April.

Examples

Ivor Crown, the dentist, makes up his accounts to 30th September.

Accounts to *30th September 1982*.
Profits taxable in *1983/84*.
Payment dates for tax in equal instalments:
1st January 1984
1st July 1984.

The time lapse between the end of the accounting period and the due date of payment of the first instalment is *15 months*.

Orson Carte, the rag-and-bone man, makes up his accounts to 30th April.

Accounts to *30th April 1982*.
Profits taxable in *1983/84*.
Payment dates for tax in equal instalments:
1st January 1984
1st July 1984.

The time lapse between the end of the accounting period and the due date for payment of the first instalment is *20 months*. Mr Carte therefore has 5 months extra time between the end of the accounting period and the due dates of payment. As pointed out previously, it will not save him tax but it may help his cash flow situation. (Refer to question 3 for details of when to pay the tax.)

What happens if I change my accounting date? 37

If you are already in business and have a year end you think may not be giving you the best tax advantages you may be considering changing your accounting date – no general advice can be given as each case *must* be examined separately. In many cases it may *not* be worthwhile because a change of accounting date means the basis of assessment of your profits is totally disrupted, which in turn can result in increased tax liabilities; before any change is made it is essential to make detailed calculations for which you will require up-to-date accounts and accurate forecasts of trading, stock levels etc.

If your profits have been reasonably static but an increase is likely in the future, it may be there is a tax saving to be obtained if the accounting date is changed. On the other hand, if profits have been high in the past and are now falling there may be scope for shortening the accounting period, especially if the original accounting date fell early in the tax year. The tax savings for this sort of venture are not likely to be enormous but they may be large enough to make it a worthwhile exercise.

What happens when my business ceases? 38

The actual date of cessation is important (as for commencing in business) as this determines the final year of assessment. If you permanently discontinue your trade, the profits assessed in the final tax year are the *actual* profits earned from the start of that tax year (i.e. 6th April) to the date of cessation. You may remember that you have the option as to what is assessed in the second and third years of assessment – this time the *Revenue have the option* to revise the previous two years' assessments (i.e. the two years before the final year, which have both been assessed on a previous year basis) to assess the *profits actually earned* during the periods, calculated on a time basis. The Revenue will elect to do this if the total profits to be assessed on an "actual" basis exceed the profits using the "preceding year" basis.

If the preceding year basis remains, part of your profits will actually not be assessed at all but this is counteracted by the fact that your first trading profit will have been assessed more than once.

The timing of the cessation is important; each case requires careful consideration of its particular facts and an accurate estimate of profits to the date you propose to cease trading. A general rule is that where profits are falling the trade should cease prior to the start of the new tax year, but if profits are rising it may be beneficial to cease early in the next tax year. In addition, there are special provisions relating to capital allowances and stock relief (see questions 42 and 44).

39 What can I do if I incur a loss in the first years of trading?

If you should be unfortunate enough to make a loss during any of the first four years of assessment from the date the trade commenced, you may make a claim that this loss be set off against your *other* income for the preceding three years, using the earlier years first. The

Revenue will want you to show that the trade was carried on during the period the loss arose, on a *commercial basis*, with an expectation of profits in the near future, and you must make your claim within two years of the end of the year of assessment in which the loss occurred. The loss set off against your other income should give you a repayment of tax.

This is a *special* loss relief for those people who suffer losses in the early years of their trading. However, you do not have to make a claim for your loss to be allowed in this way as will be seen from the subsequent paragraphs. You must therefore consider which method of dealing with your losses would prove beneficial to you.

What other ways are there of relieving losses? 40

If a loss has been sustained by you in the trade you are carrying on, this may be utilised in one of the following ways, taking into account the possibility of relief for losses in the early years of trading, as already mentioned in question 39. For these purposes "trade" also includes profession or vocation.

1 **Set off of losses against other income:** A trading loss may be set off against your other income in the same year of assessment, or in the following year of assessment provided that the trade is still carried on in the later year.

A claim must be made within two years of the end of the year of assessment in question and the loss must be set off against your other earned income, followed by your unearned income, and then in turn against your spouse's earned and unearned income, unless you make a claim to the contrary. Repayment of tax is then made accordingly.

There are further provisions if your loss is increased by claiming capital allowances or stock relief, but no loss relief will be given unless the trade was carried on for the year in question on a commercial basis, with a view to realising a profit.

2 Carry-forward of losses against subsequent years' profits: If you claim relief under the above provisions you will receive the immediate benefit of a tax repayment, but you may decide it would be more beneficial to carry all your losses forward to a later year to be set against future profits from the *same trade*. You may claim your loss relief either by setting off the loss against your other income for the year, or carrying back the loss if it was incurred in the first years of trading, but you may still have a balance – this may be carried forward instead of the full amount. There is no time limit (except as regards stock relief, see question 44) as to how many years the loss can be carried forward until it is completely used up, provided only that the same trade is still being carried on.

3 Carry-back of a terminal loss: A *terminal loss* is the amount of losses sustained in the *last 12 months of trading* when your business is permanently discontinued. These losses may be carried back and set off against the profits of your trade for the three years immediately prior to that in which the cessation occurred. Relief is given for the latest year first, then working backwards until the loss or the available profit is used up.

Beware of forfeiting your personal allowances. If your other income is low for the year in which you have a loss it may be covered by personal allowances. If this is the case do not claim for the loss to be used that year but carry it forward.

Remember: you can carry your losses forward but you *cannot* carry your personal allowances forward.

What can I claim as expenses? 41✲

Many people who are self-employed do not realise that the profit appearing in their accounts is not necessarily the same figure that will be assessed to tax. The accounts profit has to be adjusted for tax purposes as not all the expenses shown in the accounts are tax allowable. The basic rule is that *expenses are allowable if they are incurred wholly and exclusively for the purposes of the business*. Thus it follows that if an expense was incurred partly for private purposes the whole of the expenditure will be disallowed as it does not fulfil the criterion of being wholly and exclusively for business purposes.

It would not be possible to set out all the allowable or disallowable expenses and your professional advisers will be able to tell you what you can or cannot claim. You must ensure that all the expenses you have incurred during a year are included in your accounts otherwise you may pay more tax than is necessary. Below is a list of some of the items most frequently seen in statements of expenses, with a note to say whether or not it is allowable expenditure for tax purposes.

Depreciation: Not allowable, but capital allowances may be claimed (see question 42)

Advertising: Generally allowable

Remuneration: Allowable including bonuses, PAYE, cost of benefits provided, if relating to employees, not the proprietor

Entertainment expenses: Not allowable, unless for staff or overseas customers. Includes Christmas gifts

Legal fees: Not allowable if incurred while acquiring a new asset as this is part of the capital cost. Generally allowable if it is the cost of maintaining existing trading assets and rights (e.g. debt collecting)

Personal expenses: Not allowable

Rent, rates, etc., for business purposes: Allowable

Income tax payable/paid: Not allowable (except PAYE on employees' pay)

Subscriptions: Allowable if to trade or professional association

Donations: Donations to charities are allowable provided the "wholly and exclusively" rule is satisfied (i.e. there is a business or trading connection).

Travelling and subsistence: Allowable if in the course of the business activities. Not allowable are travelling expenses between home and the business address

Repairs and renewals: Expenditure on additions, alterations or improvements is capital and not allowable. Repairs (i.e. restoring something to its original condition, etc.) are allowable

Telephone: Business use only allowable

Where any such expenditure is incurred in connection with a new business in the twelve months prior to the commencement of trading, it may also be claimed as a deduction in the first year's tax assessment. In the 1982 Budget speech it was announced that the period for which this relief could be claimed would be extended to three years.

You will appreciate it is easier for a self-employed person to claim expenses in respect of his work than for an employee, whose claim may fail on the grounds it is not a "necessary" expense – as you have seen earlier (question 34).

What is the effect for tax purposes of capital expenditure? 42

If you incur expenses by acquiring a capital asset you may not deduct this from your trading profit. Assuming that the asset has a limited life span, its value to your business will gradually decline and this is anticipated by including in the accounts an amount for depreciation, but this in itself is not allowable for tax purposes. This rather strict ruling has been relaxed as there are specific allowances available against certain types of capital expenditure:

Machinery and plant
Industrial buildings
Agricultural land and buildings
Mines, oil wells and mineral deposits
Dredging
Scientific research
Patents
Know-how
Cemeteries

The first three of these categories (being the most common) are dealt with in more detail below.

It may be that a particular item of capital expenditure falls into more than one category and you would normally be able to state your preference which will obviously be to your advantage, but there are special provisions which restrict this choice in certain contexts. You must make a claim to the Revenue for the allowances but you will see it is not always advantageous to claim them. In general the granting of the allowances falls into three stages:

1 An *initial or first year allowance* of a substantial percentage of the capital expenditure: it is possible for you to claim only part of this but it would depend on the particular circumstances as to whether or not you did so.

2 A *writing down allowance* each year during the life of the asset (see later notes).

3 A *balancing charge or allowance* at the end of the trade or on the disposal of the asset. This is to bring the allowances into line with the actual amount spent: if the amount given as an allowance is less than the amount spent the difference is a *balancing allowance;* if the allowance exceeds the amount spent, the difference is brought into the income tax assessment by way of a *balancing charge.* (If the asset is sold at a profit the amount brought back into charge will not exceed the original allowances given: the excess may be charged to capital gains tax.)

The allowance is normally set against your taxable profits but if you have a loss the capital allowances can be used to increase the loss (or turn a small profit into a loss). If the allowances exceed the profit, the excess will be carried forward to future years. A word of advice – remember you cannot carry forward your personal allowances and you must consider whether or not you wish to claim the full first year allowance (for treatment of losses see questions 39 and 40).

Machinery and plant

This is certainly the most common of the capital allowances claims but as there is no definition of machinery or plant in the legislation it has provoked much discussion through the years. It includes *fixtures and fittings* but recently the Revenue are taking a much stricter view as to what qualifies; it depends on the setting of the fixture etc. in the building and whether or not it is used for the trade. An example would be the installation of a lift which would possibly be classed, not as capital expenditure for purposes of the trade, but as an improvement to the building itself. When the building is eventually sold the cost of the lift installation would be allowed for capital gains tax purposes but this does not give any immediate relief for the expenditure incurred.

The terms "machinery" and "plant" also include *motor vehicles* and these are dealt with in question 43. A few of the other rules concerning plant and machinery are as follows:

First year allowances Possible to claim allowance equal to 100% of actual expenditure, or part of it (see previous notes).

Writing down allowances If 100% first year allowance claimed this is not applicable. All plant and machinery used in the trade is grouped together into a "pool" (but see question 43 re motor vehicles). The first year it is claimed the allowance will be 25% of cost or the amount remaining following first year allowance. The net figure of the cost less the allowance is called the *written down value* – following year allowance is given of 25% of this figure and the same procedure is repeated in the subsequent years.

Leasing No first year allowance, if purchased after 1st June 1980, except in certain circumstances.

Hire purchase First year allowance on capital element at beginning of contract – no need to wait for instalments to be paid.

Industrial buildings

General rules are as follows:

1 Building must be an industrial building or structure – defined in great detail in the legislation.

2 Claimant may be a trader or a landlord, but the expenditure *must* be incurred on the construction of "an industrial building or structure which is to be occupied *for the purposes of a trade*".

3 Cost of land is excluded; private roads are included as a concession.

4 Special rules where only part of the building qualifies, where expenditure was incurred before 1962 and when the building is sold.

5 Special rules and allowances for hotels, for commercial buildings in "enterprise zones" and for "small workshops".
6 Allowances given: Initial allowance 75%.
Writing down allowance 4% of cost until fully written off.

Agricultural land and buildings
General rules are as follows:
1 Expenditure must be incurred for husbandry or forestry – proportion of the allowance can be given where appropriate.
2 Claimant may be the landlord or tenant of any agricultural or forestry land who incurs expenditure on construction of farmhouses, farm or forestry buildings, cottages, fences or other works (e.g. water supplies, drainage).
3 Apportionment of allowance applies when expenditure is on a farmhouse – one third is allowable.
4 Expenditure after 11th April 1978: initial allowance – 20%; writing down allowance – 10% of cost for 8 years.

---

43 What is the tax position on buying motor cars? If I use my own car can I claim tax allowances?

As you have already seen, motor vehicles are classed as plant and machinery but only certain types qualify for the 100% first year allowance. These are goods vehicles (e.g. lorries), vehicles unsuitable to be used as private vehicles (or not commonly used as such) and vehicles which are provided wholly or mainly for hire to the general public. If it is decided not to claim the whole of the first year allowance, the vehicles will be included in the "pool" and the 25% writing down allowance will be granted (both these terms are explained in the 'Machinery and plant' section of the previous question).

There is no first year allowance on other motor cars but if the car is bought by the business and you use it during the course of your business, the 25% writing down allowance will be granted with the car put into a separate "pool" unless it cost more than £8,000. If this is the case the writing down allowance is restricted to £2,000 each year, until the amount brought forward falls below £8,000 when the 25% rate of allowance becomes applicable.

If all the car expenses have been claimed in the accounts and these include private motoring expenses, an adjustment will be made to the taxable profit as you are not entitled to tax allowances for the private use of your car. If you use your own car for business purposes, again you may claim the writing down allowance and running expenses but they will be restricted to the business proportion only. Finally, remember that when the car is sold (whether it is owned by the business or yourself), if you have been claiming writing down allowances, an adjustment will be made in the form of a balancing allowance or charge as explained in the previous question.

What is the tax effect of increases or decreases in my year end stock valuations?   **44**

First of all the meaning of "stock" and "work-in-progress" must be understood.

Trading stock is property of any description which is sold in the ordinary course of the trade, profession or vocation, or would be sold if its manufacture were complete.

Work-in-progress is any service performed in the ordinary course of the trade, profession or vocation, part of which has been completed at the time the accounts are prepared, and for which it is reasonable to expect a charge will be made.

A form of relief to allow for changes in the level of year end stock and work-in-progress valuations was first introduced in a limited form in 1973.

For periods of account which straddle 14th November 1980, or end on or after that date, a new system of relief is in operation, having the following features:

1 Relief is calculated on the opening stock at the commencement of the period of account. For the first period of trading a notional opening stock is arrived at by "working backwards" from the first period's closing stock.

2 Relief is given by reference to percentage movements in a single index over the period of account. The index used is a specially constructed one reflecting the average prices of stocks and work in progress for the period concerned, published by the Revenue.

3 The first £2,000 of stock held by a business does not qualify for relief.

4 There will be no "clawback" of relief when stocks fall except in cases where the business ceases or the scale of its operations becomes negligible in comparison with the recent past: in such cases all relief previously claimed in the previous six years will be brought into the amount to be charged to tax.

5 There will be a restriction on the extent to which losses attributable to stock relief allowed under the new system may be carried forward after six years (see question 40(1).

6 There are special transitional arrangements for periods of account ending on or straddling 14th November 1980, so that in certain circumstances relief will be available under the old scheme if this would be advantageous. You should take professional advice as to whether these transitional provisions may be helpful.

Are there any deductions that I can claim which apply more to self-employment rather than if I am an employee? 45

You are entitled to claim all the same personal allowances whether you are self-employed or an employee. There is one relief, however, which cannot be claimed by any person who holds a pensionable office or employment (i.e. the employees are in a superannuation scheme which provides for their retirement).

The allowance referred to is *Retirement Annuity Relief* which does not only save you tax but also provides you with an annuity when you retire.

You are entitled to deduct from your "net relevant earnings" as assessed for a tax year, any premium paid under a Revenue approved annuity contract. The term *net relevant earnings* means your earnings from your self-employment (or a non-pensionable employment) having taken into account losses, stock relief and capital allowances.

You are allowed to claim a certain percentage of your net relevant earnings as a qualifying premium, depending on when you were born. From 6th April 1982 the rates are as follows:

Year of Birth	Percentage
1934 or later	17½%
1916 – 1933	20%
1914 – 1915	21%
1912 – 1913	24%
1910 – 1911	26½%
1908 – 1909	29½%
1907 or earlier	32½%

This relief will normally be given against income of the year in which the premium is paid, but it is possible to elect for a premium to be treated as paid in the previous year, or if there were no relevant earnings in that year, in the next preceding year of assessment.

A new provision was introduced in 1980 concerning "unused relief." Where the maximum amount of relief which would be available exceeds the premium paid in a year, the excess is to be treated as unused relief: this may be carried forward for up to six years and used when the reverse situation arises and the premiums paid exceed the amount allowable. Relief given in this way must be taken in the earliest possible year. *In general*, the rule to remember is that it is possible to take up unused relief before the end of six years, but that it is lost when the six year period comes to an end. However, it is possible by using the "relating back" rules mentioned above to obtain an extension. For instance, unused relief for 1975/76 should strictly be forfeited by 5th April 1982 but if a payment were to be made in the current year 1982/83, it could be related back to 1981/82 and then unused relief for 1975/76 could be set against any excess premiums in that year. (Taking the example a step further, if there were no relevant earnings in 1981/82 the payment could be related back to 1980/81 and thus take advantage of unused relief from 1974/75, which would normally have been forfeited at 5th April 1981!)

One other point concerning retirement annuity relief is the "loan-back" facility. In the past, one of the disadvantages of paying into a pension scheme was the fact that money was paid in and was not seen again until the date of retirement. Facilities are now offered, by a number of life assurance companies which allow you to "have your cake and eat it" – it is possible for you to borrow back an amount up to the level of the premiums paid, which means that the only cost need be the interest on the loan, which is charged at a commercial rate. The loan will be repaid when the policy matures, either out of the funds of the pension itself or your own personal funds.

Are there any businesses which have special rules? 46

No matter what trade, profession or vocation you are engaged in, you will find differences, possibly in what expenses are allowable, but there are certain categories which are set apart in the legislation as being treated differently. Three of these categories are discussed very briefly below:

1 Subcontractors in the construction industry: The main thing to remember in this instance is that unless you hold a subcontractors exemption certificate you will have basic tax deducted from all the payments you receive for your work. This tax is then available as a credit when an agreement concerning your tax is eventually reached, so the main disadvantage is with regard to your cash flow situation, which could be of major importance. In order to obtain a certificate, you must keep all your income tax returns, accounts and payments of tax up to date as all these things are examined closely before the issue of a certificate is authorised; it is proposed to relax some of these requirements in the case of school or college leavers who are newly starting in the industry.

2 Farmers: Basically the rules of assessment are the same as for any other self-employed person but there are a few notable differences:

Losses – unlike other trades, all farming (but not market gardening) is treated as *one* trade so that a loss on one farm may be set off against the profits of another. However, it is not possible to claim relief for the set-off of losses against other income for the same year or succeeding year of assessment (see question 40(1)) if losses were also incurred in each of the five years preceding the year of assessment concerned, except in certain circumstances.

Capital allowances – special reliefs for agricultural land and buildings (see question 42).

Stock relief – generally animals kept by a farmer are to be treated as trading stock. Where animals such as these form part of a production herd the farmer may elect for them to be treated as a capital asset – *herd basis.* (If you think this applies to your stock – seek further advice.)

Fluctuating profits – complicated rules apply but a good way of saving tax if the tests are met. Relief is by way of averaging two years' profits where there is a variance between the two years of more than 25% of the higher figure.

3 Landowners: Landowners who are not carrying on a trade are taxed on rent less expenses and this net figure is treated as unearned income (see question 24). There are also what are called "one estate" provisions in that expenses incurred on one property may be set against the rents arising on another within the same "estate" provided that certain conditions are satisfied.

---

47   What is the position if I am in partnership?

First of all it must be shown that there is actually a partnership: *an agreement to trade together and share the profits or losses* is presumed to be a partnership. The agreement does not have to be a formal legal document (in fact it can be made orally), but it is preferable to have the terms written down in some form.

Where there is a partnership, income tax is assessed on the profits of the trade or profession in the name of the partnership, although in England and Wales a partnership is not a legal entity. *Each partner is jointly liable for income tax on the whole of the profits.* Where a partnership includes a company, special rules are needed because a company, unlike an individual, is always taxed on the current year's profits: i.e. no preceding year basis of assessment.

The rules concerning the allocation of profits from a

partnership are rather involved. The partners agree for each accounting year how the accounts profit is to be divided between them – this is called the *profit sharing ratio*. However, the same profit is not necessarily divided up in the same way for tax purposes. This is because the profit sharing ratio for the income tax assessment is the ratio actually in use for that tax year and due to the preceding year basis of assessment the accounts profits for one year are not assessed until the following year, by which time the partners may have agreed to allocate their current profits differently. This is a little clearer shown in an example:

Example

Hop, Skip and Jump are in partnership. They make up their accounts to 31st March each year. The accounts to 31st March 1982 show a taxable profit of £6,000 which is divided *equally* between them. This profit will be taxed in 1982/83 (the tax year ended 5th April 1983).

Shortly after the start of their new accounting period it is decided that because Hop works so hard he is to have one half of the current year's profit (to 31st March 1983) and Skip and Jump will now take only one quarter each.

The income tax assessment for 1982/83 is based on the profits to 31st March 1982 (£6,000) and it is divided using the profit sharing ratio for the current year, to 31st March 1983. The assessment is therefore divided up as follows:

Total profit £6,000		
Hop	–	£3,000
Skip	–	£1,500
Jump	–	£1,500

although each partner was actually entitled to £2,000 for the year concerned.

It may be possible to turn this sort of situation to your advantage with careful planning and professional advice.

Partners' salaries and interest on capital are not an allowable expense for income tax purposes, being regarded as part of the partnership profits.

48 What happens if there is a change in the partnership?

In the event of any change in the partners, for tax purposes the business is automatically assumed to have ceased and a new business started at the date of the change: this would mean that the complicated provisions of commencement and cessation (see questions 35 and 38) would have to be applied. *But* if there is one partner (at least) who is a partner both before and after the change it is possible to elect for the *continuing basis of assessment* to apply. The election must be signed by all the partners both before and after the change (or an executor if necessary) and the claim must be made within two years of the date of the change – it can also be revoked during this time. It must be emphasised that the Revenue are very strict in the application of this particular time limit.

The effect of the election will be for the profits to be assessed on the normal preceding year basis, the year of change being apportioned on a time basis.

It is often beneficial to make the election and the necessary calculations should always be made to ensure that as little tax as possible is payable. It is essential to seek professional advice on this matter.

49 Part of my business is carried on abroad: can I claim any tax deduction for this?

Generally profits arising from self-employed trades or professional earnings are charged to UK tax in full, irrespective of where they arise.

However, if you spend some time travelling abroad in connection with your business it may be possible to claim a deduction for this. The relief works along the same lines as that described for overseas employments (see question 32).

If you spend 30 or more "qualifying days" (again as defined in question 32) out of the United Kingdom in any one tax year, you may claim a deduction of 25% of the profits after applying the fraction:

$$\frac{\text{number of qualifying days}}{365}$$

Unlike the employee situation, there is no provision for increasing this *pro rata* basis to take account of any special circumstances. The deduction applies to the *assessable profits* (normally computed on the "previous year" basis) of the tax year concerned.

Example

Marco Polo spent 60 qualifying days abroad in the tax year 1982/83. His taxable profits for the year ended 30th April 1981 (assessable 1982/83) were £14,000.

For 1982/83 Marco Polo can claim a deduction from his assessment of:

$$\frac{£14,000 \times 60 \times 25\%}{365} = £575$$

However, if you can establish that you are carrying on a trade or profession wholly abroad and quite distinct from any such business in the United Kingdom, and you are *domiciled and resident* (see question 32) in this country, then you can claim a deduction of 25% against the whole of the earnings from the overseas business irrespective of the number of days spent abroad. In practice this is likely to be very difficult for a sole trader to establish, but if you are a member of an *overseas partnership*, i.e. one which is managed and controlled outside the United Kingdom (and for this purpose it is essential to have at least one non-resident partner), then it will be possible for you to claim the 25% deduction against your share of the assessable partnership profits for that tax year, without any restriction for "qualifying days".

In these circumstances, if you are *not domiciled*, though *resident*, you will be liable to tax only on *remittances* of income to the United Kingdom from the overseas partnership. If you are *not resident and not ordinarily resident* then you are not liable to United Kingdom tax on such earnings at all.

---

50 Should I consider turning my business into a company?

There are several advantages to be obtained from incorporating a business but there are also many problems to be overcome. You may have derived substantial income tax benefits from the opening years of assessment rules and the special relief for losses in the early years of trading; if the profits of your business increase rapidly, making the idea of incorporating your business a good one, the additional income tax payable when adjustments are made to the closing years of assessment, together with professional fees and capital costs of starting the company, may well exceed the initial tax savings. There may be other non-tax reasons why incorporation is attractive (e.g. product liability claims). On the other hand, incorporation does not always give effective protection of limited liability (e.g. a personal guarantee to a bank), and matters such as these must be taken into consideration.

You should first of all consult with your professional adviser to discuss what would be the most suitable form of trading vehicle for your particular business. The reduction in income tax rates, and the level of National Insurance contributions payable by employer and employee, compared with the contributions paid by the self-employed, have made the decision to incorporate more difficult as the tax aspect is less obviously attractive.

With regard to the tax you are paying there will most probably be a saving of tax but this must always be compared with the actual costs of incorporating the business.

What are the advantages and disadvantages of incorporating **51**
my business?

Advantages

1 You would be able to establish a company pension scheme (to be approved by the Inland Revenue). The contributions paid by the company and the employee are tax deductible and are usually greater than the limits for retirement annuity premiums (see questions 14 and 45).

2 You may be able to make gifts of shares to utilise the annual *capital transfer tax* exemptions (see question 89). The *capital gains tax* position should not be overlooked but it may be possible to keep the chargeable gain below the taxable limit or take advantage of the general relief available for gifts (see question 74).

3 It may be easier for you to raise additional finance from banks and other third parties.

4 The benefit of limited liability can be obtained which can give valuable protection against financial risks, product liability claims and so on.

Disadvantages

1 Additional accounting and audit requirements are imposed on companies.

2 You may lose some of the flexibility of your previous business arrangements. You will be required to maintain minutes of directors meetings and other general meetings and to comply with the statutory filing requirements, the most important one being to file a copy of the accounts with the Companies Registration Office each year. Such filed accounts are available for inspection by any member of the public.

3 Once you become a director of a company rather than a participant in an unincorporated business (whether by yourself or in partnership) you are then subject to the very strict rules concerning benefits and expenses, and your drawings from the company are subject to PAYE – which can cause cash flow problems.

4 If you have a husband and wife partnership with a flexible profit sharing agreement this will have to cease if the business is incorporated. The agreement may have meant your spouse was given a material slice of the profits, to utilise personal allowances and the lower rates of tax, although he or she perhaps did not take a very active part in the business. Once the business becomes a company the remuneration paid will be reviewed by the Inland Revenue more critically and if it is considered to be excessive for the duties actually undertaken, the Inspector may not allow a part of the salary paid for corporation tax purposes.

---

52   How does incorporation actually affect my income tax position?

The transfer of your business to a company is treated as a cessation of the unincorporated business and the special rules for the final years of trading will apply (see question 38). The timing of the incorporation therefore requires careful planning if increased income tax assessments are to be avoided.

There are special rules concerning stock relief, capital allowances and losses, and it may be possible to avoid any clawback on stock relief allowed, or balancing charges on capital allowances given. These rules are complicated but can result in useful tax saving. The incorporation of a business is something you should *not* consider without professional advice.

IV
Keeping Good Company
TAXATION OF THE COMPANY — CORPORATION TAX

What are the basic rules of corporation tax (including rates of tax, reliefs, dates for payments, special rules etc.)?   53 ✹

The first and perhaps the most obvious rule, is that corporation tax is only paid by companies. A company means any *body corporate or unincorporated association* but does not include a partnership, a local authority or a local authority association. There are special rules and exemptions for certain types of companies, including charitable companies, unregistered friendly societies, trade unions, scientific research associations, and for certain nationalised industries. To be liable to pay corporation tax a company must be *resident* in the United Kingdom and it will then pay tax on all its profits, wherever they arise. The residence of a company does not necessarily depend on where the trade is carried on: it is resident where its controlling board of directors meets (and not simply where the directors are resident) and from where the company is controlled and managed on a day-to-day basis. *Non-resident* companies are only subject to corporation tax if they are carrying on a trade through a branch or agency in the United Kingdom; but if this is the case they are then taxable on the profits arising from that branch or agency.

Unlike income tax assessments on individuals and sole traders, corporation tax is not troubled by the preceding year basis of assessment. Corporation tax is assessed on a company for its *accounting period*. The accounting period for tax purposes is normally the same as the company's period of account: it is sometimes necessary to determine an accounting period in instances where the company commences or ceases to trade in a period of account, or the period of account is longer than a year. An accounting period *cannot* exceed 12 months, so where the company prepares its accounts for a period of more than 12 months there will be two accounting periods for tax purposes, one for 12 months and the other for the balance, the profits being allocated on a time basis. If, therefore, the company has an 18 month period of account, there will be an assessment raised on the first 12 months on 2/3rds of the profit, and the second assessment will be made for six months, on 1/3rd of the profit.

Corporation tax is assessed, not in the income tax year from April 6th, but in respect of the *financial year, to 31st March*. So, if an accounting period straddles that date, the profits have to be apportioned between two financial years, and taxed accordingly. The rate of tax is fixed in arrears – the rate for the year ended 31st March 1982 is 52%; the rate for the year ended 31st March 1983 will not be known until the 1983 budget.

There is also a *small companies rate* which for the year ended 31st March 1982 is set at 40%. This applies to companies whose annual profits do not exceed £90,000. However, there is a *marginal relief* where the profits are between £90,000 and £225,000, which is calculated by a special formula. Where the profits exceed £225,000, the whole amount is subject to the full rate of 52%.

The tax is normally due nine months after the end of the accounting period, or if the assessment is made late within 30 days of the date the assessment is issued. The exceptions to this rule are the companies which were trading on 1st April 1964, when companies were still paying income tax. They will continue to have the same interval from their accounting date to the due date for payment, as they did under the old income tax rules. If the tax is paid late the risk is run of incurring an *interest charge* as for income tax (see question 3), but on the other hand if there is a corporation tax refund due from the Inland Revenue, if certain tests are satisfied there may be a *repayment supplement* also due, again with similar rules to income tax (see question 3).

You may have heard the term *close company* which is applied to a company that is controlled by five (or fewer) of the main shareholders, or by its directors. (This is over-simplifying the position – the rules to decide whether a company is close or not are very complicated.) In recent years, the legislation was such that if a company was close it could lead to problems as the law required a certain amount of the income of these companies to be distributed each year, and there was also a much wider view of what constituted a distribution made by the company. However, the latest legislation has greatly relaxed the rules relating to close trading companies, for accounting periods ending after 26th March 1980, and therefore there should not be any problem in the future. If you have a problem with an accounting period ending before that date, you should seek professional advice.

What are the profits of a company? Are they computed in the same way as for income tax? 54

The *profits* of a company include both *income* and *chargeable gains*. The amout of income is, in general, computed in accordance with income tax principles; if those principles should be changed during an accounting period, those in force at the end of the period are applied. You should always make sure that *all possible claims for expenses* are made to reduce the profits as much as possible. The taxation of chargeable gains is dealt with separately (see question 60).

A company is not entitled to personal reliefs and allowances as these are only available to individuals.

55   What are charges on income and how are they dealt with?

Charges are comprised chiefly of annual interest, royal-
ties, and payments under charitable deeds of covenant.
Classed as charges on income they are allowed as deductions against the *total profits* of the accounting period in
which they are *actually paid*. A payment does not rank as
a charge on income if it is deductible in computing
income from a particular source, thus interest payable to
a bank is generally treated as a trading expense and not as
a charge on income.

Charges on income (other than bank interest) must be
paid under deduction of tax at the basic rate and the
company must pay this income tax over to the Collector
of Taxes.

Where there are charges on income consisting of payments made wholly and exclusively for the purposes of a
trade carried on by the company, and these plus other
charges on income exceed the total profits of the company, then whichever is the *smaller* amount (out of the
charges incurred exclusively for the trade or the excess of
charges over profit) is treated as a trading expense and so
becomes entitled to *loss relief*. Losses incurred in this
way can only be carried forward, they cannot be carried
back to a previous accounting period.

**56   Can my company claim stock relief in the same way as an
individual or partnership?**

Stock relief *can* be claimed by companies in the same
way as individuals or partnerships (see question 44).

**57   Can my company claim allowances for capital expenditure in
the same way as an individual or partnership?**

Again, the rules for claiming capital allowances are much
the same as for individuals and partnerships (see question 42). There is *one important difference*, in that if losses

are increased or actually arise from claiming a *first year allowance* in respect of plant or machinery, the trading loss arising from such a claim can be carried back up to *three years* (which generally would lead to the re-opening of an earlier year and a repayment of corporation tax).

If my company incurs losses, how can they be utilised?   **58**

Where a trading loss arises in a company there are a number of ways in which relief for it may be obtained:
1 The trading loss may be carried forward to be set against future profits from the *same trade*.
2 Alternatively, the trading loss may be set against other profits of the same period, including chargeable gains.
3 The loss may be carried back for one year and set against profits from all sources provided the company was trading during that period.
4 Losses may be carried back for up to three years if created by a claim for first year allowances (see question 57).
5 Trading losses incurred by a company which is a member of a group can be passed to another member of the group (see question 65).
6 Trading losses incurred in the last 12 months of trading (i.e. a terminal loss) can be carried back for up to three years.
7 Allowable expenditure incurred in the twelve months before trading commenced may be claimed as an expense in the first accounting period. As announced in the 1982 budget, this is to be extended to three years.

As a director of the company, is there any advantage in reducing the profits by drawing more remuneration?   **59** ✳

If your company is incurring trading losses each year there is no advantage in voting the directors further fees or bonuses, etc, for this will only result in each individual paying income tax on the bonuses and the company increasing its losses, which it possibly cannot utilise.

But on the other side of the coin, it is always advisable to ensure that the directors have used all their personal allowances, even if this is only increasing the loss – there may come a year when the company makes a profit and can utilise its losses; once the individuals' personal allowances have been forfeited, they *cannot* be reclaimed.

The situation to consider now, is what to do if your company is making a profit. *The company will pay tax at either 40% or 52%* (if its profits are sufficiently high): *you, as an individual and director of the company, start paying tax* (after your allowances have been granted) *at 30% and you will not pay tax at 40% until your taxable income exceeds £12,800.*

To take it a step further, if your company is paying tax at 52% you may have a taxable income of up to £25,300 before your own tax rates exceed 50%.

This is obviously a *very important point* to consider when your profits are known – a great deal of tax can be saved by voting commission at the right level to the directors. *Beware*, however, that fees or bonuses are not voted to a director who plays very little part in the day-to-day running of the business, as this may be challenged by the Inland Revenue and possibly disallowed for corporation tax purposes.

---

60   What is the capital gains tax position of a company?

A company pays corporation tax on its profits and for these purposes *profits includes chargeable gains*. The gains are computed in the same way as for individuals who pay capital gains tax (see question 67), but only a fraction of the gain is included for the calculation of profits. The present fraction is 15/26ths, which, together with a corporation tax rate of 52% gives an effective rate of 30% on the whole of the gain – perhaps this is more clearly expressed if the figures in the fraction are doubled – 30/52nds.

The small profits rate of 40% cannot be applied to capital gains; in addition, capital gains cannot be used to relieve trading losses brought forward, nor a terminal loss carried back.

If a company incurs a trading loss it may carry the losses forward against future trading profits, or the loss can be set against profits of the same accounting period, no matter what the description: a *trading loss may therefore be set off against gains of the same accounting period.* However, the reverse cannot happen – a capital loss cannot be set against trading profits but can only be set against current or future capital gains.

Remember: the company may also claim rollover relief (see question 81).

What are the tax consequences if my company pays a dividend? 61✳

Persons owning shares in a profitable company may look for some return on their investment in the form of a periodic dividend on their shares. This is usually paid yearly or half-yearly and the amount will depend on what the directors consider is available out of the profits of the company for distribution in this way. This can apply particularly where some of the shareholders are not directors and therefore draw no remuneration from the company; otherwise it is not uncommon for family private companies not to pay any dividends at all (though this can sometimes lead to problems with non-trading companies or companies with substantial investment, as distinct from trading income).

If your company pays a dividend it is also required to make a payment of "advance corporation tax" (ACT) to the Revenue within certain time limits. The name derives from the fact that the company is entitled to offset payments of ACT against its liability to corporation tax on its profits, primarily those of the accounting period in which the dividend is paid. This set off may be subject to certain restrictions and to the extent that it cannot be fully used then, the surplus may be carried back for relief for a period of up to two years or carried forward indefinitely.

The purpose of the tax is to ensure that the dividend can be treated as income in the hands of the recipient which has already suffered tax. Thus when the shareholder receives his net dividend he is also regarded as being entitled to a "tax credit" (equivalent to the corresponding ACT) which is taken into account in his own tax settlement. The current (1982/83) rate of ACT is 3/7ths of the amount of the dividend: this corresponds to the present basic rate of income tax of 30% on the "gross equivalent", i.e. the dividend plus tax credit. The operation of this may be illustrated as follows:

Example

Norah Bone Ltd is a company specialising in the sale of canned dog food. In the year ended 31st December 1982 the company made taxable profits of £300,000 before tax and on 31st July 1982 it pays a dividend of £35,000 to its shareholders.

Its corporation tax portion for the year would be:

Profits chargeable to corporation tax	£300,000
Corporation tax at 52% (say)	£156,000
Dividend paid	£ 35,000
ACT thereon at 3/7ths	£ 15,000
(= 30% of £35,000 + £15,000)	

The company would actually account for its corporation tax liability in two parts as follows:

ACT due 14.10.82	£ 15,000
Balance ("mainstream liability") due 1.10.83	£141,000
	£156,000

If a shareholder received out of this dividend £7,000 he would be entitled to a tax credit of 3/7ths of £7,000, i.e. £3,000. If, because of other income, he is effectively liable to income tax at a rate of 75% on this income, he would have additional tax (known as "excess liability") of £4,500 to pay for the tax year 1982/83, calculated as follows:

"Gross equivalent", i.e.	£10,000
Income tax thereon at 75%	7,500
Less tax credit	3,000
	£ 4,500

This further tax would be due on 1st December 1983 or 30 days after the issue of the notice of assessment if this is later (see question 2).

On the other hand if the shareholder was not liable to tax at all on this income, for example because it was a charity, then it could reclaim the whole of the tax credit of £3,000 from the Inland Revenue.

The question has referred only to *dividends*. However there are other categories of payments in money or money's worth called *distributions* which are liable to ACT in the same way. In particular where shareholders take assets, e.g. stock, out of the company at less than market value, the undervalue is taxed as if it were a dividend. A similar result follows where shareholders put assets into a company at an overvalue. Transfers between a company and its shareholders do therefore need to be looked at carefully with this aspect in mind.

Where a company receives a dividend (or distribution) from another UK company, it is *not* liable to any corporation tax on that dividend. However it cannot use the tax credit that goes with that dividend, except against any liability to ACT on dividends that it in turn pays. A set off in this way does reduce the eventual amount available for credit against the company's corporation tax liability.

62 When and why is a receiver or liquidator appointed to a company?

Ever since man first began to trade there have been businesses which have failed, so this is not a new phenomenon, but over recent years there has been a marked increase in the number of bankruptcies and petitions for winding-up, by far the greater number of these being smaller businesses.

If a business fails it is said to be *insolvent* but this is something which is not defined. It is not just a matter of liabilities over assets, so a certain amount of subjective judgement is necessary. It has been said that there appears to be nothing wrong in the fact that directors incur credit, when they know the company is not able to meet all its liabilities as they fall due, but what is most definitely wrong, is if the directors continue to incur credit when it is clear the company will *never be able to satisfy its creditors*.

The main areas with regard to corporate failures are *receiverships* and *creditors liquidations;* the latter may be either a voluntary liquidation or a compulsory liquidation. Either way there is normally a formal appointment of a person to take control of the assets and business of the company.

A *receiver* may be appointed by a major creditor, e.g. a bank, to protect the security of its outstanding debt. A receiver, on taking appointment, becomes the agent of the company but this does not suspend the directors of the company, although in practice it will curtail their powers. The appointment will not alter the beneficial ownership of the company itself of its assets or business.

Should the directors prove unable to maintain that the solvency criteria are met, steps must then be taken to commence formal liquidation proceedings. Normally these take the form of a creditors *voluntary winding-up* which involves summoning a meeting of shareholders to pass a winding-up resolution. Not more than one day later a meeting of creditors must be held (called at the same time as the shareholders meeting) and they should confirm the view of insolvency and appoint a liquidator. As an alternative to this, particularly if urgent action is required, the directors of the company may apply to the Court for a *compulsory winding-up order*, which will probably be provisional and subject to a later confirmation. (Proceedings started in this way tend to be more formal and a good deal slower.) Occasionally, when a liquidation follows a receivership, the assets of a company may be negligible and if the company cannot find an individual willing to act as liquidator (because there is little likelihood of him being paid) the role of the liquidator may be undertaken by the Official Receiver (an officer of the Department of Trade).

It is important to remember that liquidations have different implications to those of receiverships. The latter (i.e. receiverships) can be temporary interruptions in a company's business but the appointment of a liquidator is the forerunner of the dissolution of the company.

What happens if a receiver is appointed to my company?   63

When a receiver is appointed to a company, he will most probably have to make some quick decisions concerning the assets of the company and whether or not to continue trading: the commercial decisions will obviously take priority over any tax planning. However, it is possible, depending on the timing of those decisions, to obtain substantial tax benefits for the company even while it is in receivership. The appointment of a receiver does not, by itself, give rise to any tax consequences for the company (unlike the day a liquidator is appointed) and tax on profits and other income is still the responsibility of the company during this period.

The main aim during receivership must be to utilise losses of the company and the receiver should obtain the following information:

1 the extent of the tax losses brought forward
2 the trading forecast for the current period
3 the possible effect of realising assets
4 the possible effect of the company ceasing to trade
5 the scope for recovering tax under a terminal loss claim.

These decisions can only be made when each case is considered on its merits; the timing of cessation of trade may be critical, in view of the terminal loss claim which could be made (to be carried back for three years). If the receiver finds out the position early enough, he may be able to take the necessary steps to make the best use of the tax losses available, and arrange, where possible, for the company to obtain the maximum benefit of taxation relief, prior to the point of time when a winding-up may become inevitable.

---

64 What happens if a liquidator is appointed?

If a liquidator is appointed, the directors lose their powers, the company ceases trading and it is effectively the end of the employees' existence. The liquidator is concerned only with realising what assets remain so as to meet the claims of the various creditors.

If the receiver has done his job well the date of the winding-up *may* be planned to obtain a tax advantage. When the resolution is passed for the winding-up of a company, the current accounting period comes to an end and a new one commences. Future accounting periods then end on each anniversary of the winding-up.

A liquidator is not personally liable for the company's tax liabilities in respect of the period before the commencement of the winding-up, but he is required to meet them out of the company's assets. During the period of liquidation it is his responsibility to pay the tax – this even ranks in priority before his own remuneration! Some of the creditors of the company are described as *preferential creditors* and one of these is the Inland Revenue. This means that tax will be paid in preference to other outstanding debts and it includes corporation tax, advance corporation tax, capital gains tax, income tax and development land tax, but normally only for one year. The choice as to which year's assessment (should there be more than one outstanding) is to rank as the preferential debt, is left to the Inland Revenue. Any other tax liabilities normally rank with the other unsecured creditors to share in whatever assets may be left.

Should my company stay on its own or become a member of a group?   65

The decision whether to run a business through one company or through a group of companies, is dependent upon many factors, not all concerned with taxation, but nevertheless there are taxation aspects to be considered. A company carrying on trading activities is subject to corporation tax, and if those activities are divided up between different companies, even if they are all part of a group, *each company is treated separately, with its own profits and therefore its own corporation tax liability*.

There is no charging of the group as a whole on its total profits, but there is relief which may be claimed in a number of ways:

1 Dividends paid to a parent company may be paid without advance corporation tax.

2 Interest and other annual payments may be paid between group companies without deduction of income tax.

3 A parent company may pass any surplus advance

corporation tax (see question 6) down to a subsidiary which can then use it, subject to certain restrictions, against its own liabilities to corporation tax.

4 Certain assets may be transferred within the group without incurring a liability to capital gains tax.

5 All the trades carried on by members of a group are treated as one trade for the purposes of rollover relief for capital gains tax purposes (see question 81).

6 Trading losses and other deductions may be passed to another member of the group by what is called "group relief".

There are different rules for each category of relief depending on whether the subsidiary is a 51% or 75% subsidiary of its parent; there are also special provisions concerning stock relief, capital allowances and value added tax (see question 100).

✸66 Can I set up a company overseas and what would be the tax position?

There is a certain amount of freedom if you should wish to set up a company overseas; there is no rule to say that the profits of an overseas company are to be treated as those of its parent company, resident in the United Kingdom, so this would seem to give great scope for tax planning. *Beware*, however, of the stringent "anti-avoidance" rules which specifically prohibit the transfer of a trade to an overseas (non-resident) company without obtaining Treasury consent. It is unlawful for any company resident in the United Kingdom to become non-resident without Treasury consent, and the rules concerning this are very detailed. Consent will be given if a commercial purpose in transferring the trade or opening a subsidiary can be shown, plus a net benefit to the United Kingdom balance of payments. Linked with these rules are other provisions which prevent avoidance of income tax by transactions which result in the transfer of income to persons who are resident abroad. *There are severe penalties for failing to comply,* and it is essential to obtain detailed professional advice if any transactions of this kind are contemplated.

It is proposed to make substantial changes in this legislation and this is at present being considered.

Non-resident companies are only liable to pay corporation tax if they are carrying on a trade through a branch or agency in the United Kingdom – the advantages of transferring the trade overseas as mentioned above are therefore obvious. If the trade is carried on by a branch or agency in the United Kingdom, the company will pay tax on its profits, including the following:

1 trading income from the branch
2 income from property or rights held by the branch
3 gains accruing from the disposal of assets of the branch or agency, in the United Kingdom.

A non-resident company cannot be a close company (see question 53) but sometimes capital gains realised by the company are attributable to the shareholders. A non-resident company cannot be a member of a group of companies for United Kingdom tax purposes.

If a company which is resident in the United Kingdom, but trading overseas, transfers part or all of the trade and assets connected with that trade to a non-resident company so as to show a profit on the transaction, and the consideration received consists partly or wholly of shares and/or loan stock in the company acquiring the trade or asset, the charge to tax on the gain may be postponed. The purpose of this rule is to acknowledge that the gain is primarily a gain on paper only, and gives the company time to acquire the funds to pay the tax; in other words it is a form of rollover relief. The postponement is subject to certain rules, and lasts until the recipient company disposes of some or all of the assets (during six years) or the company who transferred the assets disposes of some or all of the shares it received in return.

In the same way as for individuals (see question 25), where income is taxed in both the United Kingdom and overseas, it is usually possible to obtain relief for the overseas direct tax by way of credit against the corresponding United Kingdom tax, through the provisions of the appropriate Double Tax agreement.

V
Some You Win – Some You Lose
CAPITAL GAINS TAX AND THE INDIVIDUAL

What is capital gains tax? What are the rates of tax and do I   67 ✳
still pay capital gains tax if my gains are not substantial?

Capital gains tax, first introduced on 6th April 1965, is a completely separate tax from income tax. The basis of charge to this tax can be stated as follows: *when a chargeable person disposes of a chargeable asset, either a chargeable gain or an allowable loss will arise.*

You are a *chargeable person* if, during a tax year (i.e. during a year ending on 5th April) you dispose of a *chargeable asset* and at any time during that year you are resident in the United Kingdom. There are special rules if you do not normally live in the United Kingdom or if you are domiciled outside the United Kingdom (see question 32); if this is the case you should seek further advice. If you die, all your chargeable assets will be treated as disposed of, but death is *not* an occasion of charge for capital gains tax purposes.

Any form of property, in the widest sense, and whether situated in the United Kingdom or not, can be a *chargeable asset.*

In simple terms there is a *chargeable gain* if the proceeds you receive on disposal of an asset exceed the cost of the asset at the date it was acquired. Similarly, if the proceeds on disposal are less than the cost of the asset at acquisition, an *allowable loss* will arise.

This has meant, in recent years, that individuals selling assets have paid tax on what is an artificial gain as no account has been taken of inflation.

This has now been changed and, with effect from 6th April 1982 (1st April for companies) the acquisition value of assets disposed of will be increased by the appropriate amount by reference to the retail price index (RPI). This adjustment will reduce or extinguish a gain but it will not be allowed to create a loss where there would otherwise have been a gain. It will not apply at all to losses. Relief will not be given for the first year of ownership so that short term gains will not be reduced by indexation. For other gains the adjustment will not start until the end of the first year. The RPI increases are to be measured from March 1982 or, if later, from the end of the first year of ownership. These new rules are better illustrated by examples:

1 An asset acquired in September 1970 and disposed of in October 1985 will only qualify for an increase in its acquisition value by reference to the movement in the RPI between March 1982 and October 1985

2 An asset acquired in September 1982 and disposed of in October 1985 will qualify for an increase by reference to the movement in the RPI between September 1983 and October 1985.

In addition to this relief there is also an annual exemption. If your aggregate chargeable gains do not exceed £5,000 for 1982/83 you will not pay any capital gains tax. For 1983/84 onwards it is proposed that the amount of the exemption should be indexed, by the same percentage as the increase in RPI for the December preceding the year of assessment, over the previous December.

You should therefore consider carefully when making disposals: if you wish to realise a large sum of money by disposing of your assets, by spreading this over two years it is possible there could be a substantial saving of tax. *Remember, you will not pay any capital gains tax if you keep the gains below the specified amount each year*. Refer also to question 76 dealing with losses.

If your chargeable gains do exceed £5,000 you will pay tax at 30% on the excess.

For trusts, capital gains are free of tax if they do not exceed £2,500; if they are in excess of this figure tax will be charged at 30% on the excess.

For 1981/82 and previous years the chargeable gain was calculated by comparing the figures for acquisition value and disposal proceeds, and applying the manual exemption (£3,000 in 1981/82) to the gain arising, and charging tax at 30% on the balance.

Are any assets exempt from this tax? 68

Gains arising on the disposal of certain assets, as set out below, are exempt from capital gains tax; by the same token any loss arising on their disposal is not allowable for these purposes.

Chattels: These are assets which are touchable ("tangible") and moveable. They are exempt if the disposal is for £3,000 or less. (A special computation is necessary if the sum exceeds £3,000.) This does *not* apply to currency (but see under "Foreign currency" below). There are also special rules dealing with "sets" of chattels. Prior to the 6th April 1982, the exemption was limited to £2,000.

Motor cars: These are not chargeable assets unless they are of a type not commonly used as a private vehicle and unsuitable to be so used.

National Savings Certificates, Premium Bonds etc.: These, and other government securities which are not transferable, are exempt whenever they are acquired or disposed of.

Government securities ("Gilt-edged"): These are exempt if held for more than 12 months.

Betting and other winnings: Betting winnings are not chargeable gains and rights to winnings obtained by any pool betting or lottery are not chargeable assets. Premium Bond winnings, etc., are also exempt.

Foreign currency: Exempt when disposed of providing it was acquired only for personal and family expenditure.

Medals and decorations: Exempt unless acquired by purchase.

Compensation for damages: Exempt if received for personal or professional wrong or injury; if the damages etc. relate to an asset, payment will constitute a disposal.

Life assurance policies and deferred annuities: Exempt when disposed of or realised by the original policyholder but *not* when disposed of or realised by another person who may have acquired them by subsequent purchase.

---

69   Is my home a chargeable asset?

In general, if your dwelling-house is your only or main residence throughout your *period of ownership* there will be no charge to capital gains tax when you sell the property: this exemption extends to the building and (in most cases) up to one acre of land.

However, you may at some time during your period of ownership be required to live elsewhere, through the terms of your employment for instance, or a period of working abroad, in which case your claim that the house is exempt can be affected. The following periods of absence (i.e. the time you are *not living* in your house) do *not* affect your claim, providing you live in the house for a period both before and after (except for 5 below) the specified periods of absence:

1 In any circumstances, a period or periods not exceeding three years.

2 A period during which you are employed abroad.

3 A period, or periods, not exceeding four years during which you are prevented from living in the house by reason of the location of your work, or a condition by your employer requiring you to live elsewhere.
4 The first 12 months of ownership prior to taking up residence during which the house is being built or alterations made.
5 The last two years of ownership are exempt, regardless of whether or not you are living there.

The periods of absence mentioned are also ignored where husband and wife are living together and the conditions are satisfied by the spouse who is not the owner. Where the conditions for exemption from capital gains tax are not satisfied throughout the period of ownership the gain is apportioned on a time basis.

If, as a result of a breakdown of marriage, one spouse ceases to occupy the matrimonial home and later transfers it to the other spouse who has continued in occupation, no gain will be chargeable.

What is my position if I own more than one property?　　70

You are only allowed to have one dwelling house at a time for the purposes of the exemption referred to in question 69. If you have more than one house available for your residence at the same time you may choose which one is to be treated as your main residence. A chargeable gain will arise on the disposal of the other property and you should therefore seek advice regarding the value of each – this way it is hoped the smaller of the gains arising will be charged to tax, by electing for the property giving rise to the larger gain to be exempted as your main residence. Notification of your decision may have effect for up to two years before the date of notice and will continue until varied by a further notice – if you do not make a choice the Inspector of Taxes will make it for you: if you disagree with his decision you have the right to appeal (i.e. object) with a view to asking his agreement to your own choice. If you acquire a dwelling house for the sole purpose of selling it again at a profit there is no exemption from capital gains tax, even though you may live in it for a period.

If the property is used as the residence for a dependent relative of yourself or your spouse and he or she occupies the house rent-free, this property will be exempt from capital gains tax, *in addition* to your own main residence. Relief must be claimed from the Inspector of Taxes and it is given in proportion to the part of the period of ownership during which the house is occupied by the relative. *Note:* This exemption can only aply to *one* dependent relative per marriage (or per claimant, if he or she is single).

There is also exemption from capital gains tax if you are the owner of a property as the personal representative or trustee of a deceased person. There are certain special rules and if you consider that this may apply to you, it is advisable to ask for further advice.

✳71   Does it make any difference if I let my house or take paying guests?

You may wish to supplement your income in a tax year by taking a lodger into your home; if he lives with you as part of your family, sharing the living accommodation and taking meals with you, this will *not* affect the exemption for capital gains tax when you sell the property.

If, however, you let part of your home to a paying guest, depending on how much of the home is let (i.e. how many rooms etc.) and for how long, the exemption may be restricted. If you disposed of a house which had been part let *before* 5th April 1980 there was no relief for that part of the house. If the sale occurs *after* 5th April

1980 there is relief on the let portion of the house, but this must not exceed the amount of exemption due on the rest of the house. This relief is only given up to a maximum of £10,000 in any case.

How am I affected if I use part of my house as an office? 72

If you are employed by a firm who expects you to work at home, you may have been advised to claim an income tax allowance for the use of a room in your home as an office (see question 18). Similarly, if you are self-employed you may also have to use part of your home as an office. If part of your house is used *exclusively* for business purposes you may lose the exemption from capital gains tax on that part of the house. You should therefore take care *not* to set aside part of your home exclusively as an office – *be sure that the room you use is also used for other private purposes*.

Are gifts chargeable to capital gains tax? 73

A gift of an asset is a disposal for capital gains tax purposes: however, if you are making a gift there are obviously no sale proceeds, so the chargeable gain is computed by substituting (for sale proceeds) the *market value of the gift* at the date it was given. (For these purposes the market value is the price which the asset might reasonably be expected to fetch if it were sold on the open market.)

There are certain gifts which are completely exempt from capital gains tax:
1 transfers between married persons living together
2 gifts of assets not exceeding £100 in a tax year
3 gifts of cash in sterling
4 gifts to charities

5 gifts of land, buildings and chattels to the National Trust and other similar bodies, and of works of art etc., given for the national benefit.

✱74   If I make a gift which is not exempt from capital gains tax, is there any relief I can claim?

If the gift is not exempt the chargeable gain will be assessed, and the person making the gift (i.e. the donor) would normally pay the capital gains tax due. From 6th April 1980 if the gift is made to an individual resident in the United Kingdom the gain can be *held over*. This means that instead of the *donor* paying the tax, the gain will be deducted from the acquisition value of the gift; this in turn means that the *donee* (i.e. the person receiving the gift) will pay the capital gains tax (subject to any exemptions that he may be able to claim) when the asset is eventually sold, as he has a *lower* acquisition value to be deducted from the sale proceeds, leaving a *higher* chargeable gain. Both the donee and the donor must elect jointly for this relief to apply.

With effect from 6th April 1981, this "holdover" relief is also available for gifts made to a trust.

A useful point for you to remember (although perhaps rather macabre), is that death is not an occasion of charge for capital gains tax purposes, so that if an asset is given to a donee who subsequently dies, if both parties signed an election for this "holdover" relief to apply there will be no capital gains tax to pay on that gift.

NB: if, although it is a gift, the donor actually receives consideration from the donee in respect of the gift, there may be some capital gains tax to pay and the above relief will be restricted accordingly.

Can I save tax by claiming expenses? 75

If you incur expenditure when acquiring or disposing of an asset this can be used to reduce the chargeable gain. Expenses which are allowable fall into the following categories:

1 Costs incidental to the acquisition: these may only be deducted if they are actually incurred by the person acquiring the asset. They must be incurred *wholly and exclusively* for the purpose of the acquisition; this would apply to fees, commission, cost of transfer etc., together with advertising costs incurred in finding a seller.

2 Improvements: again the expenditure must be incurred *wholly and exclusively* in respect of the asset, this time to enhance its value. Such expenditure *must* be reflected in the state or nature of the asset at the time of its disposal.

3 Establishing rights to the asset: expenditure is allowable if it is incurred *wholly and exclusively* for the purposes of establishing, preserving or defending your title to the asset. This is a very strict rule and operates narrowly.

4 Costs incidental to the disposal: these are defined in the same way as the costs of acquisition and cover legal fees and the cost of advertising to find a buyer. Costs reasonably incurred in making or finding a valuation for capital gains tax purposes will also be allowed.

General investment advice and expenditure on financial journals are *not* allowable.

If I make a capital loss, can I turn this to my advantage? 76 ✳

You will no doubt have realised by now that it is to your advantage to keep your chargeable gains below the figure of £5,000. The treatment of losses incurred in both the current and previous years can play an important part in reducing your chargeable gains to this figure.

Losses realised in the current year must be set off against gains for the current year as far as it is possible to do so, and any excess may then be carried forward. However, *losses brought forward* from a previous year need only be set off against current year gains to the extent necessary to reduce those gains to £5,000. The benefit of this is two-fold, as you are still able to carry any excess losses forward but you have also been able to utilise the tax free band of the first £5,000 gains.

Losses brought forward from previous years are therefore of obvious importance, and if you are approaching the end of a tax year with no realised gains it may be possible to create losses by *bed and breakfast* transactions (see question 77) to build up a bank of losses to carry forward to future years. *A word of warning:* if you have already realised gains in the current year, "bed and breakfast" transactions to create losses should only be carried out in order to remove the gains from the taxable threshold, as any current year losses which reduce the gains to below £5,000 will effectively be wasted.

As a general rule you cannot set your capital losses against your other income and if you are in business you cannot set trading losses against capital gains, but it is possible to claim the set-off of a loss arising on the disposal of shares in an *unquoted* trading company, against your other income for income tax purposes *provided* the shares were acquired by subscription in cash or money's worth and not actually bought from a previous shareholder. The share must *never* have been quoted on the Stock Exchange, and there are other tests to be satisfied before the relief is given.

Another general rule concerning losses is that they may not be carried back to be set against gains of an earlier year; there is an exception to this in the year of death when losses can be carried back for three years, covering the later gains first.

If you make a disposal of an asset to a *connected person* and incur a loss, that loss may only be utilised against gains arising from future disposals to the same person, if he or she is still connected with you. As an individual you are "connected" with any relative of yourself or your spouse, and the spouse of any of those relatives. If you are a trustee you are "connected" with the settlor and any other person or body corporate connected with the settlement. Finally, if you are in partnership you are "connected" with each partner and their respective spouses and relatives.

There is also loss relief in respect of a *qualifying loan* – see question 81.

What is a bed and breakfast transaction? 77

A *bed and breakfast* transaction will normally apply to quoted shares and securities. There is a practice on the Stock Exchange whereby shares may be sold on one day and repurchased the following day. The time to sell is when the quoted price is considerably lower than the price you purchased them for; this has the effect of creating an allowable loss to be set against other gains (see question 76).

You must remember that reacquiring the shares at a low value is all very well, but if the price rises, when you sell you may incur a large chargeable gain: however you have already achieved the advantage of creating a loss to set against other gains, and if you finally sell the shares when you have little or no gains for a year of assessment you will not be liable to pay any capital gains tax if you keep your annual gains below the limit. It is therefore possible not only to defer tax, but to actually save paying any at all.

It is also possible to realise a gain by a bed and breakfast transaction by selling at a time when the quoted price is higher than your purchase price. This could be useful if you have losses brought forward to a tax year which can be used to cover the gain so you will not pay any capital gains tax, and you will then go forward with a higher cost of the shares to be set against the sale proceeds when you make the eventual sale, thus reducing the final charge to capital gains tax.

The introduction of some relief for inflation from April 1982 described in question 67 may make arrangements of this kind less attractive.

✳78   **If I am married how does this affect my capital gains position?**

The rules concerning husband and wife are as follows:
1 Transfers of assets between spouses who are living together are regarded as made on a basis of *no gain, no loss*. (The exceptions to this are on death or the transfer of trading stock to or from either spouse.)
2 The house of husband and wife living together – see questions 69 and 70.
3 The capital gains and losses are calculated for each spouse separately; excess losses of one are available to be set against gains of the other except where there is an election to the contrary (see 5 below).
4 The net gains and losses are assessed jointly on the husband (unless an election is made to the contrary), except for the year of marriage when the wife is assessed as if she is a single person, unless the marriage took place on 6th April. If the tax remains unpaid by the husband the Inland Revenue may press for payment by the wife, up to the amount she would have to pay if a separate assessment election was in force.
5 Either party to the marriage may claim for separate assessment for capital gains tax if they make application

before 6th July in the year following the end of the year of assessment. There is the same time limit for revoking such an election. The total payable is to remain unchanged but the wife will have an assessment on her own gains and she is therefore liable to pay her own tax.

6 The £5,000 exemption from capital gains tax applies as if it is divided between the spouses living together, in proportion to their respective taxable amounts, or, where these amounts total less than £5,000 and there are losses brought forward from previous years, in such proportions as they agree.

There is only limited scope, therefore, for saving tax as a husband and wife team, for capital gains tax purposes. The advantages are that the exemption of the first £5,000 may be split between you in whatever porportion you choose. This can in certain circumstances preserve the losses of one spouse, to be carried forward, although against this, the other spouse may pay tax in the current year.

Children who are minors are entitled to their own exemption limits which gives scope for future reduction in a family's capital gains tax burden if transfers of part of a family shareholding are made to the children at any early stage – if this should create a loss, refer to the rules on "connected person", covered in question 76.

I have assets which I acquired before capital gains tax was introduced (on 6th April 1965). What is the position on these?   **79**

There are two answers to this question depending on whether assets are quoted shares and securities, or unquoted shares or property. The rules governing each category are as follows:

Quoted shares and securities: Two computations of the gain/loss are necessary when the shares are sold. The first is of the difference between the selling price and the original cost of the shares, the second is of the difference between the selling price and the market value of the shares, as quoted on the Stock Exchange on 6th April 1965: the smaller gain or loss is accepted when the computations are compared. If one computation shows a gain and the other a loss the disposal is treated as a "no gain – no loss" situation.

These rules also apply to land held on 6th April 1965 which is subsequently disposed of at a price including development value.

Other assets including unquoted shares and land without development value: Here the gain/loss is calculated on a "time basis", to and from 6th April 1965. Capital gains tax was not introduced until that date, and it follows that you should *not* be taxed on any gain arising *before* that date. The computation is the sale proceeds less the acquisition cost which gives an overall gain deemed to have arisen evenly over the period of ownership. The gain is then apportioned to and from 6th April 1965 and only the latter part is charged to tax after any relief for inflation (see question 67) or other exemptions. (If the asset was acquired before 6th April 1945 the gain is only calculated from the 1945 date, but still using the original cost.)

Again, there are provisions to make an election for the market value at 6th April 1965 to be used in place of the original cost, in which case there is no time-apportionment (the gain is sale proceeds less market value). The election is irrevocable and must be made within two years of the end of the year of assessment in which the disposal is made. Unfortunately, the Revenue will not discuss a valuation until an election has been made, which could mean you end up paying tax on a higher figure than if time-apportionment was used – and there is then nothing you can do.

It is important to refer all matters concerning such assets held on 6th April 1965 to a professional adviser,

who will be able to advise whether or not an election for
the 6th April 1965 value will be to your advantage.

What are paper for paper transactions and how do they affect my capital gains position? 80

If you hold shares in a public company you may have
realised that some transactions do not involve the actual
buying and selling of shares. For instance, the company
may decide not to distribute its profits as dividends, but
to capitalise part of them (perhaps to build up reserves),
in which case there may be a *bonus issue* of additional
shares to the existing shareholders, for which they pay
nothing. On the other hand, a company seeking to
increase its capital by an issue of new shares may allocate
some of the new shares at a preferential price to its
existing shareholders. This is referred to as a *rights issue*.
In the *reorganisation of a company's capital*, blocks of
shares may be exchanged or two companies may *amal-
gamate* or *merge* (or one company may *take-over* another)
by the exchange of share capital. In none of these situations are you buying shares in the normal way.

For the purposes of capital gains tax, if you acquire
shares through any of the above circumstances, this is
not classed as a chargeable occasion. The new or
increased holding is, on the occasion of a later disposal,
treated as having been acquired at the same time and at
the same cost (plus any payments made for "rights"
issues) as the original holding.

In some instances you will be given the new shares
automatically (e.g. "bonus" issue), but with the "rights"
issues you are able to make a choice as to whether or not
you take up the new shares. If you decide not to take up
the offer you may then "sell the rights" to the new
shares, for a (usually) relatively small consideration.
This is a chargeable occasion, but if the amount you
receive does not exceed 5% of the market value (on that

day) of the shares you already hold, there will be no charge to capital gains tax at that time: the amount received is deducted from the total acquisition cost of the holding, which increases the gain on an eventual disposal.

If the transaction offered by a company means you receive a capital distribution in money or money's worth (possibly in addition to the shares offered), which is not treated as income, you are then treated as having disposed of a part interest in the shares you hold and a gain is then calculated using only a proportion of the acquisition cost as the base cost for this purpose.

✱ 81   Are there any other reliefs for which I may qualify in certain circumstances?

The following few brief notes concerning other reliefs are not a comprehensive guide. The rules are complicated and if you consider that you may qualify for relief under any of these headings you *must* seek further advice.

Rollover relief: A trader, disposing of assets used exclusively for the purposes of his trade, *who applies sale proceeds in purchasing assets to be used for a trade,* may elect to defer capital gains tax, by deducting the amount of the chargeable gain arising on the sale of the old asset, from the acquisition cost of the new asset. The purchase of the new asset must take place within one year before, or three years after, the disposal of the old asset, but these time limits may be extended at the Revenue's discretion.

If only part of the sale proceeds is used to purchase the new asset, there is a corresponding loss of relief. Furthermore this relief is only given on any gain remaining when *retirement relief* (see below) has been taken into account.

Retirement relief: This relief applies where the individual is over 60 years of age and disposes of whole or part of a business which is owned by him, or shares and securities in his "family" company. There are many conditions to be satisfied concerning the transaction and past history of the business or family company, but if these are fulfilled throughout a maximum qualifying period of ten years, relief will be given to its full extent. For periods of less than ten years a proportionate reduction is made, on a time basis, so that the minimum "relevant percentage" is 10%, based on a minimum period of one year. Further, relief is given concessionally if, in association with a sale of shares in his family company, the individual also disposes of an asset owned by himself that has been used by the company – again there are certain conditions to be fulfilled.

The relief is for persons aged over 60 years of age; the maximum amount being £50,000 for claimants 65 or over, reduced by £10,000 each year for claimants aged between 60 and 65 (this is normally computed using years and months rather than complete years). The relief is then given against the part of the gain relating to "chargeable business assets" (which means further calculations) and the relief is then subject to the percentage reduction mentioned above.

Qualifying loan, loss relief: First of all, it must be established for this purpose, what constitutes a *qualifying loan*.

The loan must have been given, after 11th April 1978, to a resident of the United Kingdom for use wholly in his trade (so the borrower may also be a company), profession or vocation. The provisions do not apply to borrowings in the form of loan stock or any other similar marketable security; losses on these may be claimed in the normal way.

Provided the Inspector of Taxes is satisfied that the claimant and the borrower were not spouses living together (or companies in the same group) and that the lender has not assigned his right of recovery, he may allow loss relief to the extent that any part of the capital element of the loan has become irrecoverable. If, at a later date following a loss claim, all or part of the sum is recovered, a chargeable gain will arise on the claimant.

---

82   When do I pay my capital gains tax and are there any other administrative details I should know?

Capital gains tax will become due and payable on *1st December following the end of the year of assessment* to which the gains relate, or 30 days after the issue of the notice of assessment, whichever is later. It is therefore possible to make a disposal on 6th April 1982 (or after) on which the capital gains tax will not be due until 1st December 1983, at the earliest.

If you disagree with the assessment you have the same right to appeal as for income tax and the same provisions also apply for request for postponement of part of the tax charged, interest on unpaid tax and payment of a supplement on tax repayments (see question 3).

Where the consideration to be paid in respect of an asset you have sold is paid to you by instalments, it is possible for you to *pay tax by instalments* over a period not exceeding eight years, if you can satisfy the Revenue that to pay all the tax in one sum would cause you hardship.

Finally, do not think that if the Revenue does not know of the gains you have made you will not have to pay the tax. You should notify the Revenue of your gains within one year of that year of assessment, and there are *penalties for failure to do so* – see question 4.

VI
Capital Ways of Saving Tax
CAPITAL TRANSFER TAX

What is capital transfer tax? What are the rates of tax and when am I liable to pay it? 83❋

Capital transfer tax was introduced in 1974 to replace estate duty, which only taxed assets passing on death and certain lifetime gifts. This tax is charged on *the value transferred by a chargeable transfer* whether it is made during a lifetime or on death. A *transfer of value* is, broadly, anything which results in a reduction to the person making the transfer; the *value transferred* is the resulting fall in value in the estate of the person making the transfer, and a *chargeable transfer* is any transfer of value made by an individual after 26th March 1974. For capital transfer tax purposes *estate* means the aggregate of all the property to which you are beneficially entitled.

Unlike capital gains tax, for the purposes of this tax, *death is an occasion of charge*. There are two separate scales for the rates of tax, one for transfers made during your lifetime and the other for all your property which is transferred on the event of your death. There is an added sting in the tail as any transfers you make in the three years prior to your death, are charged at the "death" rates, which are considerably higher than the "lifetime" rates – credit is given for tax already paid. Remember that this is a *cumulative tax* and your transfers are therefore added to each other, year by year.

This may present a rather black picture but perhaps the situation is not as bad as it first seems; *you do not start paying the tax until your chargeable transfers have totalled £55,000*, this being in addition to the annual and other exemptions covered below (see questions 89 and 90). *For the purposes of this tax husband and wife are treated separately so you will each have a total of £55,000 chargeable transfers before you pay this tax.*

Furthermore, for transfers made on or after 10th March 1981 the cumulative principle applies only to transfers in the ten years before the transfer in question, in determining the amount of tax to be paid on that occasion. This has the effect of reinstating the £55,000 non-chargeable band every ten years.

The £55,000 exemption limit applies from 9th March 1982 (prior to this the limit was £50,000), as do the rates shown in the tables below. It is proposed that with effect from 6th April 1983 the threshold at which the tax becomes payable and the subsequent rate bands should be adjusted in line with changes in the retail price index.

Transfers made during your lifetime:

Portion of value		
Lower limit	*Upper limit*	*Rate of tax*
£	£	%
nil	55,000	nil
55,000	75,000	15
75,000	100,000	$17\frac{1}{2}$
100,000	130,000	20
130,000	165,000	$22\frac{1}{2}$
165,000	200,000	25
200,000	250,000	30
250,000	650,000	35
650,000	1,250,000	40
1,250,000	2,500,000	45
2,500,000	—	50

Transfers made on death or within 3 years before:

Portion of value Lower limit	Upper limit	Rate of tax
£	£	%
nil	55,000	nil
55,000	75,000	30
75,000	100,000	35
100,000	130,000	40
130,000	165,000	45
165,000	200,000	50
200,000	250,000	55
250,000	650,000	60
650,000	1,250,000	65
1,250,000	2,500,000	70
2,500,000	—	75

These rates apply to transfers made on or after 10th March 1981. Prior to that date substantially higher rates applied to lifetime transfers. The advantage of making lifetime transfers as distinct from the position at death is clearly seen.

Does it make any difference where I live? **84**

If you are *domiciled* in the United Kingdom (see question 32) you will be liable to pay capital transfer tax on all your assets irrespective of where they are situated. If you are domiciled abroad tax is still payable, but only on any assets you have situated in the United Kingdom. The meaning of domicile is discussed in general terms in question 32 but this is extended for capital transfer tax purposes. In many situations *it is possible to be caught for capital transfer tax, even if for other purposes it is accepted that you have abandoned your United Kingdom domicile.*

85 Can I make a transfer without it being a transfer of value?

If certain conditions are fulfilled, you may be able to show that a transfer you have made is not a transfer of value and so no capital transfer tax is payable. The transfer is *not* a transfer of value if it was not intended to be for the benefit of any other person, and it was to a person or persons not connected with yourself. If the transfer was to a person connected with you (e.g. a member of your family or a business partner), it must also be shown that it was made on the same terms as would have applied had it been made to a complete outsider. Other transfers which may not be chargeable to this tax include:

1 Expenditure to maintain the family (including illegitimate children and children not living with their own parents but who have been with the transferor for long periods).

2 Waiver or repayment of remuneration, provided that it would have been assessable on the recipient under PAYE, and allowed as a deduction in computing the profits of the payer (e.g. the company).

3 Waiver of dividends, provided this is done within 12 months before the right to the dividend accrued.

4 Expenditure which is allowed for income tax purposes.

86 Who pays the tax on a chargeable transfer?

The persons liable to account to the Inland Revenue for the tax on a *lifetime transfer* are:

1 the transferor
2 the transferee
3 any other person in whom the property is vested or who has an interest in possession
4 any other person who benefits from the property.

The persons liable for the tax on *death* are:

1 the personal representatives of the deceased

2 any person in whom the property is vested after death

3 as regards tax arising on settled property – the trustees of the settlement

4 again for settled property – any person who benefits from the property after the death.

The persons liable for the tax on chargeable transfers from a *settlement* are:

1 the trustees of the settlement

2 any person who is entitled to an interest in the capital or income of the settlement

3 any person who benefits from the settled property

4 if the trust has trustees who are not resident in the United Kingdom – the settlor during his lifetime.

The persons mentioned above in 1 of each paragraph are the persons primarily liable to pay the tax in each case. *Remember that it could be advantageous for the donee to pay the tax* – if you as the transferor pay the tax, added to your cumulative chargeable transfers will be the amount of the transfer *plus* the tax; if the transferee pays the tax, he will receive a smaller net amount, but your total transfers will only be increased by the actual amount of the gift.

In the event of the death of the transferor within three years of making a transfer, the additional capital transfer tax liability will be payable by the transferee. It is possible for this to be paid out of the estate, but only if the terms of the will or codicil allow.

When is the tax payable and is there any way to delay payment? 87✳

The due date of payment of this tax varies depending on whether it is a lifetime transfer or a transfer made on death. *For lifetime transfers* the due date is six months after the end of the month in which the chargeable transfer was made, or 30th April in the tax year following that in which the transfer is made, whichever is the later. It is therefore possible to make a transfer in the early days of a tax year and not be liable to pay the tax until after the end of that year (a possible 12 months); however, if you wait until later in the tax year you will only have six months in which to pay. Interest (nondeductible for any tax purpose) runs from the due date.

For transfers made on death the tax is due within 12 months of the end of the month in which death occurred, but interest will start to run six months from the end of the month in which death occurred.

The rate of interest on tax paid late on lifetime (or settled property) transfers is 12%. The rate is 9% if the charge is on a transfer at death or it is the additional tax due on a transfer made within three years of death.

It is possible to pay the tax by instalments if it is either a transfer at death or a lifetime transfer where the transferee is paying the tax. These provisions only apply to certain property transferred: basically this includes land, shares which gave the transferor control of any company immediately prior to the transfer, and certain unquoted shares. If this relief is allowed, tax is paid by eight equal annual or 16 equal half-yearly instalments. The first payment is due six months from the end of the month of transfer. If the "instalment property" is sold while instalments are still outstanding, the balance of the tax is payable immediately.

---

88 What are the alternatives if I do not have the necessary funds available to pay the tax?

If you cannot obtain the necessary funds to pay the tax, the Revenue may accept the following property to pay the tax as a payment in kind: land; buildings, and contents associated with those buildings;pictures, prints, books, manuscripts, works of art, scientific objects or other items, or collections of such items, if of national scientific, historic or artistic interest.

Can I make gifts without adding to my cumulative chargeable transfers? 89

There are three categories of gifts which are not chargeable to capital transfer tax; remember these are for *lifetime transfers:*

Annual exemption: The first £3,000 of transfers each tax year is exempt; any unused relief can be carried forward for one year only, against transfers in excess of the limit for the later year. Unless there is a regular pattern of making gifts, so that these take place at least every other year, some of the benefit of this exemption may be lost.

"Small" gifts: The first £250 of transfers to any one individual in each tax year is exempt. Unused relief cannot be used in a later year: the exemption only applies to outright gifts, not to settlements. This is in addition to the annual exemption (as mentioned above). It is therefore possible to pay any number of people £250 in a year and not have made a chargeable transfer. However, the relief cannot be used to cover the first slice of a larger gift; thus a transfer of £1,000 would be covered by the annual exemption, leaving £2,000, and could not be covered by the £250 small gifts exemption so as to use only £750 of the annual exemption.

Gifts in consideration of marriage: Transfers made in consideration of marriage are exempt, but only within set limits which vary according to the degree of affinity between the transferor and the parties to the marriage. If the transferor is a parent of one of the parties to the marriage, he may give £5,000; if the transferor is a more remote ancestor he may give £2,500; if the transferor is one of the parties to the marriage the limit is £2,500; anyone else may give £1,000. For this exemption it is important to ensure that there is evidence that the gift is actually made in consideration of the marriage. The gift should be completed *before* the marriage; unless special steps are taken, such a gift cannot be effectively made after the marriage.

You will see from all this that substantial amounts can be transferred without capital transfer tax being paid. *It can only be to your benefit to take advantage of these exemptions.*

✱ 90   Apart from the gifts mentioned in question 89, are there any other exempt transfers I can make?

There are other types of transfer which are exempt from capital transfer tax but you may not think of them as gifts, in the same way you would think of the gifts already mentioned. These are listed below and apart from the first (normal expenditure out of income), they apply to the deemed transfer on death as well as to lifetime transfers:

Normal expenditure out of income
If a transfer is effected out of income it may not be relevant to capital transfer tax. To qualify for this exemption, three conditions must be satisfied:

1 transfer is made as part of the normal expenditure of the transferor

2 transfer is made out of his income (comparing one year with another)

3 after allowing for all such transfers the transferor is left with sufficient income to maintain his usual standard of living.

The expenditure must be "habitual" and the Revenue will look for a pattern of payments made to the same person. The expenditure must involve cash outlay; gifts of assets will only qualify if they were bought for the purposes of making the gift. "Income" is taken as net of income tax for these purposes.

Transfers between husband and wife
A transfer between husband and wife is generally exempt, except where the spouse receiving the transfer is domiciled outside the United Kingdom. If this is the case only the first £55,000 will be exempt (£50,000 prior to 9th March 1982).

Where one spouse has a large estate and the other has not, tax can be saved by topping up the smaller estate to make sure both parties receive the benefit of the lower rates of tax. *This is an area where careful planning can save a great deal of tax* and professional advice should be sought to ensure the right arrangements are made.

Charities
Lifetime transfers to charities are initially exempt but if, having made a transfer you should die within 12 months, the exemption is restricted to £250,000 (£200,000 prior to 9th March 1982). The same limit applies at death but this is also reduced by the amount of gifts to charity made in the last year of life. The charity pays any tax becoming due in this way.

Political parties
If you should wish to make a donation to a political party, this will be exempt from capital transfer tax as a lifetime transfer, with similar rules to charities for the 12 months prior to death and bequests at death. The maximum to be exempt in this event is £100,000.

A political party only qualifies if it has two MPs or it has one MP and gained 150,000 votes at the last General Election.

National heritage
There are three different exemptions in this category, i.e. gifts for national purposes, gifts for public benefit and conditional exemption.

1 Gifts for national purposes: transfer is exempt if it becomes the property of specified bodies – certain museums, galleries and trust funds are specified by name (e.g. National Trust); similar national institutions

may be approved by the Treasury; many museums and art galleries maintained by local authorities and government departments are also included.

2 Gifts for public benefit: transfer is exempt if it is property which then becomes the property of a non-profit-making organisation, provided the Treasury gives its consent. The property so transferred may be land, buildings, works of art, etc, and the Treasury will be looking for items of outstanding scenic, historic, scientific, architectural or aesthetic value, as appropriate. The Treasury may require undertakings to preserve the asset and to provide reasonable access to the public.

3 Conditional exemption: the property involved in this relief is basically the same as for gifts for the public benefit. The transfer is conditionally exempt to the extent it is attributable to property designated by the Treasury. The property remains in private ownership and the Treasury will require various undertakings to be given before the exemption is allowed. Capital transfer tax becomes payable if there is a breach in the conditions or if the property is sold, unless the undertakings are renewed. This is only the brief outline of this relief and if you wish to claim, you should seek further advice.

---

91   What is excluded property?

Excluded property is not included in your estate either for the purpose of lifetime transfers or in the event of your death. Excluded property includes the following:

1 property situated outside the United Kingdom if the beneficial owner is domiciled abroad (see questions 32 and 84)

2 a reversionary interest (i.e. something which reverts to you) providing it is *not* purchased by you

3 certain government securities beneficially owned by

persons not domiciled or habitually resident in the United Kingdom (see questions 32 and 84)

4 national savings owned by persons domiciled in the Channel Islands or Isle of Man

5 property passing as a result of death in active service

6 pash options under approved annuity schemes

7 overseas pensions

8 property owned by members of visiting armed forces.

If I have made chargeable transfers are there any reliefs I can claim?   92 ✳

The following gives a few brief notes with regard to reliefs which may be available if you have transferred a particular form of property, or the circumstances are unusual; this is *not* a comprehensive guide and if you consider you may be eligible for any of the following you should seek further advice.

Business property relief: Basically this relief provides that if you transfer "relevant business property" the value transferred will be reduced by a percentage which will vary depending on the type of business property concerned. The relief can be claimed whether the transfer is made during your lifetime or at death, and there is no limit to the value transferred which can qualify for this relief.

Relevant business property includes:

1 a business or interest in a business (reduction 50%)

2 shares/securities in a company which was controlled by the transferor immediately before the transfer (reduction 50%)

3 non-controlling shareholdings in a company where the shares are not quoted on a recognised stock exchange (reduction 20%)

4 in *certain* circumstances, land or buildings, machinery and plant used for business purposes (reduction 30%)

There are many conditions to be satisfied before the property is eligible for relief.

Agricultural property relief: This relief applies to transfers made during your lifetime or at death, and provides that if the value transferred is attributable to the agricultural value of agricultural property in the United Kingdom, owned by working farmers, the *value may be reduced by one half of the agricultural value*.

Where the land is let, for transfers made after 10th March 1981, the landlord may claim a reduction at 20% of the agricultural value; there was no relief available prior to that date.

Relief for woodlands: A claim can be made that the value of trees or underwood growing on land in the United Kingdom (which is not agricultural property) be left out of account in determining the value transferred on the owner's death. Relief is to be claimed, by the person who would be liable to pay the capital transfer tax, during the two years following the death, but this time limit may be extended. The basic condition to be satisfied is that the woodlands must have been owned by the deceased for five years prior to his death. There will be no charge to capital transfer tax unless the woodlands are disposed of either by sale or gift so it is possible to extend the relief through a succession of deaths.

Mutual transfer relief: Relief is available where the recipient of a lifetime gift then makes gifts of equal or lesser value back to the original transferor. The transferee may be able to make the return gifts free of capital transfer tax if he fulfils certain conditions. If the return gift is not made within twelve months of the original gift, the value returned is reduced by 4% for each complete year since the original gift. The maximum period available for a mutual transfer is therefore 25 years from the original gift.

Voidable transfer: Capital transfer tax is repayable in respect of any transfer which is subsequently declared void by an enactment or rule of law, e.g. bankruptcy.

How is my estate calculated at my death and are there any   **93**
further reliefs my personal representatives can claim?

Your "estate at death" holds basically the same meaning
as your estate during your lifetime; it includes all the
property of whatever description to which you are beneficially entitled. An exception to this is life assurance
policies which are included in the estate at their full
value. At death your estate will also include all property
contained in a settlement if you had an interest in the
capital or income of the trust, but there are exceptions to
this rule.

There are circumstances in which a relief from part of
the tax due at death can be claimed. When a person dies,
and his estate is chargeable to capital transfer tax, if the
estate is increased by a chargeable transfer which had
itself given rise to a capital transfer tax liability within the
previous four years, the personal representatives may
claim what is called *Quick Succession Relief*. The amount
of relief given is a percentage of the previous capital
transfer tax charged depending on the time between the
date of the previous transfer and death.

How are my assets valued?   **94**

If you refer back to question 83 you will see it states that
capital transfer tax is chargeable on a *transfer of value*
which is, broadly speaking, the fall in value of the estate
of the person making the transfer. To be more specific
this is called the *loss to the donor*, so if the donor is paying
the tax on a lifetime transfer, this must also be taken into
account as part of the reduction in the estate. The value
of the item transferred must therefore be *grossed up* to
include the tax payable, to arrive at the total transfer of
value, which becomes part of the cumulative transfers to
date. If the donee pays the tax, only the value of the gift is
brought into the cumulative total.

On death, only the actual value of the assets included in the estate is charged to tax and there is no "grossing up"; but refer to question 93 with regard to life assurance policies.

For many forms of property, the value will be an obvious amount, or relatively easy to calculate, but problems occur when *valuing unquoted shares* because a hypothetical situation must be used – this involves a hypothetical sale in a hypothetical open market between a vendor and purchaser both of whom are also hypothetical! This principle for valuing unquoted shares has been built up over recent years, but it has long been established that the larger the holding, in general, the greater the price it should command. In certain circumstances adjustment may be made to the open market value in arriving at the amount of capital transfer tax or capital gains tax, so there may be material differences between the valuations applied to the two taxes.

Shares beneficially owned by (a) husband or wife, (b) any trust in which either spouse has an interest in the income or capital or (c) any charity as the result of a gift made by either spouse after 15th April 1976, are *related property* for capital transfer tax purposes (but not capital gains tax). Any *related property is then treated as a single holding* for valuing any transfer made by the husband or wife (but *not* if the transfer is made by the discretionary trust or charity). It follows therefore that although the separate shareholdings of husband or wife may only be minority holdings, when taken together they may constitute a majority holding, and it is as part of the latter that the capital transfer tax valuation must be considered.

Note: for transfers made prior to 10th March 1981, shares held in a discretionary trust made by either spouse before 27th March 1974 also had to be taken into account as "related property".

Is it possible to change arrangements made by a will after the death has taken place, and if so, what are the tax consequences? 95

It is possible to change arrangements made by a will by what is called a *deed of family arrangement* which effectively permits a deceased person's will to be re-written after his death and any capital transfer tax will then be calculated as if the original will had been written in the same terms as the deed. For capital transfer tax and capital gains tax purposes the charge is effective from the date of death, but for income tax purposes it is only effective from the date of the deed.

The deed must be entered into within two years of death, by an instrument in writing, and the persons doing so must notify the Inland Revenue within six months. The point of making such a deed would be lost if additional capital transfer tax became payable, but if this is the case, the persons liable to pay the additional liability (i.e. the personal representatives) must be among the persons making the instrument.

All persons who may benefit under the original will must agree to the making of a deed of family arrangement if it affects their interests. This may not be feasible where the interests, even quite remote, of infant beneficiaries are involved. It is essential to obtain expert legal advice on the possibility of entering into such arrangements.

96 **If I create a settlement, will I pay more tax? Will the trust also be liable to pay capital transfer tax? If so, are there any trusts which are exempt?**

The creation of a settlement will affect your personal capital transfer tax position, as the very act of creating the settlement will involve a chargeable transfer and as such will be treated in the usual way, being added to your cumulative transfers over the years and taxed as appropriate.

Trusts have been attacked by the legislation on all sides – not only income tax and capital gains tax but also on the capital transfer tax front. There are many different kinds of trust, but in most cases capital transfer tax is payable where there is a distribution of capital. This can be as a result of the death of the life tenant, by the trust coming to an end or a variety of other reasons. For some trusts, there is also a periodic charge every ten years, commencing every tenth anniversary of the establishment of the trust falling after 1st April 1983. Trusts are not something which can be dealt with, except to give a very brief outline, in a book of this kind. *There are, however, certain trusts which, if set up properly, need not pay capital transfer tax.*

Accumulation and maintenance trust: The following conditions *must* be met:

1 One or more persons will become entitled to an interest in possession (which may be absolute or need only be an interest in the income) on or before attaining the age of 25.

2 Income is accumulated unless used for the maintenance, education or benefit of a beneficiary.

3 Not more than 25 years have elapsed since the creation of the settlement, *or*, all beneficiaries are grandchildren of a common grandparent.

If the trust qualifies, the periodic charge will not be payable and no further capital transfer tax arises when a beneficiary attains his interest.

Protective trust: This would come into force in the instance where the principal beneficiary attempts to assign his interest to someone else. This would give the trustees discretion over the income but the periodic charge would not be payable even on the subsequent death of the principal beneficiary.

Trust for the mentally disabled: There is no capital transfer tax payable if the trust is created for a mentally disabled person, and regardless of who the settlor is, periodic charges are deferred until the death of the mentally handicapped person.

Charitable trust: Trusts which are wholly charitable are not subject to the normal rules, and they are exempt from the periodic charge and tax on all distributions.

Employee trust: For a trust of this type to qualify for any form of deferment of tax, the beneficiaries must be restricted to persons of a class defined by reference to employment, persons married to those so defined, or charities. Payments to beneficiaries are not classed as a capital distribution, and the periodic charge is deferred until a capital distribution payment is made.

If I am a trustee and must therefore pay the tax, are there any reliefs I can claim? 97

You are allowed to claim some of the reliefs which are available to individuals as follows:

1 gifts to charities and major political parties (see question 90)

2 gifts for national purposes (see question 90)

3 gifts for the public benefit (see question 90)

4 Quick Succession Relief on death (see question 93)

VII
The Indirect Tax You Must Pay
VALUE ADDED TAX

✱ 98 **When do I have to register for VAT and is there any tax planning to consider?**

Value added tax is a form of indirect taxation and as such perhaps you had not previously thought of this as an area where you could possibly save tax.

One of the most important features of VAT is registration: VAT is to be accounted for by *taxable persons* who make *taxable supplies*, or supply *taxable services* in the United Kingdom, during the course of their business. A taxable person is someone who makes or intends to make taxable supplies while he is registered. The point at which you are liable to be registered is governed by various turnover limits, but if you are an "intending trader" or your turnover falls below these levels, you may register voluntarily, at the discretion of the Customs and Excise office.

If you have just started in business the date or point at which you should register is clearly important. Output tax can be an unexpected expense but perhaps even more important, if you are not registered for VAT purposes, you cannot reclaim the input tax you have paid on goods and services supplied to you; this would be most important in the earliest days of your business before you are obliged to register for VAT purposes, although under certain circumstances it may be possible to reclaim tax on goods or services supplied prior to registration. The limits of turnover should be kept under review: these are currently £6,000 at the end of a quarter but £17,000 over a whole year.

If, at the end of a quarter, your turnover exceeds the limit, you will be required to register unless it is agreed that the annual limit will not be exceeded; tax will then be chargeable from the 21st day following the end of that quarter. Failure to get all this right can result in a great deal of unnecessary expense – if at any time the Customs and Excise office think the annual limit might be reached you will be ordered to register immediately and tax may be assessed from an earlier date.

If I am registered for VAT, what happens if there is a change in my circumstances? 99 ✳

After you have registered for VAT purposes, if there is any change in your circumstances you *must* inform your local VAT office and there are penalties for failure to do so. Many of the possible changes which could occur will require the *deregistration* of your business, which must be notified to the VAT office within ten days of the change. The most important circumstances are as follows:

1 The business is closed down or sold.
2 The proprietor of the business takes one or more persons into partnership.
3 A partnership ceases to exist but one of the former partners becomes the sole proprietor of the business.
4 A company is incorporated to take over a business previously carried on by a sole proprietor or partnership.
5 A business previously carried on by a company is taken over by a sole proprietor or partnership.
6 Taxable supplies cease for any other reason.

A business may apply to deregister for VAT purposes if its annual turnover is expected to fall below £16,000.

When your registration is cancelled you may be awaiting either tax invoices for services already provided to you, or the completion of services relating to the business you carried on when you were registered. If so, you may not be able to claim input tax on these services in your final VAT return, but you may be able to claim a special repayment.

Other changes in circumstances may be dealt with by a simple amendment to your registration (e.g. address, change in the trading name of the business, etc.).

---

100   **Is there any way I can plan to minimise the tax charge and are there any special rules if my business is a company?**

There is no way to minimise the actual tax charge whether your business is a company, a partnership or you are the sole proprietor. However, as the implications of VAT accounting are more connected with cash flow, if you are a trader who regularly claims a repayment you will be allowed to make a monthly return rather than the normal quarterly return. The actual format of your accounting records can give rise to planning considerations, for example in the case of dealers in certain categories of second hand goods, such as motor cars or works or art, where the Customs and Excise regulations are particularly strict. Similarly retailers who deal mainly in cash, and who do not normally issue tax invoices, have a choice of several schemes which are aimed at arriving at a calculated figure of output tax. If you are a retailer it is clearly very important that you select the scheme most beneficial to you, so you should always take professional advice when setting up in business.

If your business is a company, generally it is taxed under the same rules as a sole trader or partnership but the one thing to remember is that if your company is a member of a group of companies it may be beneficial to be registered as a group and not as separate companies. The arrangements for which companies are to be included and which are not are very flexible, and an application can only be refused by the Customs and Excise office if it is necessary for the protection of the revenue.

VIII
The Range of
Possibilities

The present Government is committed to encouraging
investment in businesses and to assist industries and
areas where there are special problems. The existing
business opportunities programme promoted by the Government is being widely publicised to ensure that
everyone is aware of what schemes and assistance may be
available. Two such measures which may be of particular interest are the *business start-up scheme* and the
loan guarantee scheme.

The *business start-up scheme* was introduced in 1981/82
to encourage private investors not otherwise connected
with the business to make an investment in a new business; subject to certain conditions, the investor can
obtain tax relief on the amount he has invested. The
scheme is to run until 5th April 1984 and the maximum
amount allowable for tax relief each year is £20,000. For
1981/82 this limit was £10,000 and any unused balance
of this amount at the 5th April 1982 can be added to the
following year.

Secondly, *the loan guarantee scheme* was devised to
help people to start in business and this was also introduced in 1981/82. The Department of Industry, in con-
junction with the major banks, will provide guarantees
of up to 80% of the amounts advanced on approved
ventures, up to a maximum of (currently) £75,000;

interest is charged at a commercial rate with an additional premium to cover the guarantee.

In addition there are also various incentives available in particular areas of business, for example the construction industry and agriculture, and in particular parts of the country, for example development areas and enterprise zones.

You will by now have realised that the title of this book is not stating a fact; the ways of saving tax are *not* limited to 101, for there are endless possibilities to be considered. Indeed, if you were to count the reliefs, allowances, pieces of advice and so on given in these 100 answers you would find they totalled well in excess of 101! However, you must remember that this book cannot supply you with *all* the answers – it can only draw your attention to matters to which more detailed care and attention should be given. Always seek professional advice on any taxation (or other financial) matter about which you are not clear.

IX
Special 1983 Budget Supplement and Checklist

This fully-updated supplement deals with the changes in tax rates, allowances, incentives, etc. which were announced by the Chancellor of the Exchequer in his Budget speech on 15th March 1983. The opportunity has also been taken to refer to a number of developments of interest to taxpayers which have come out since the 1982 Budget.

Each bold marginal number cross-refers to the questions in the main body of the book.

The *personal tax rates* announced for 1983/84 are as follows: **1**

Rate %	Taxable income in £'s
30	1 – 14,600
40	14,601 – 17,200
45	17,201 – 21,800
50	21,801 – 28,900
55	28,901 – 36,000
60	over 36,000

The limit for the *investment income surcharge* for 1983/84 is **2**
raised to £7,100; the rate on the excess is unchanged at 15%.

The rate of interest payable on overdue tax and allowed on **3**
refunds was reduced to 8% with effect from 1st December and 6th December 1982 respectively.

5   The *personal allowances* are increased for 1983/84 as follows:
single person   £1,785

6   The tax allowances for certain children were finally phased
out in the tax year 1981/82.
married person   £2,795

9   wife's unearned income allowance   £1,785

These changes represent increases of about 14%, well in
excess of the amounts required by the indexation provisions
mentioned in question 5.

11   The limits for *small maintenance payments* mentioned in
paragraph 4 on page 15 apply to payments made by one
party of the marriage to the other party for the latter's
maintenance or to any person under 21 for his or her own
benefit, maintenance or education. Where payments are
made to any person for the benefit, maintenance or education of a person under 21, the limits are £18 per week or £78
per month.

12   The *additional allowance* for single parent families is
increased to £1,010 for 1983/84.

14   The limit for pensionable earnings (paragraph 5 on page 19)
is increased to £12,220 for 1983/84.

15   National Insurance contributions and limits for 1983/84
have been fixed as follows:

Class 1:	lower earnings limit	£32.50 per week
	upper earnings limit	£235 per week
Class 2:	flat rate contribution	£4.40 per week
	small earnings exemption	£1,775
Class 3:	flat rate contribution	£4.30 per week
Class 4:	6.3% of net profits between £3,800	
	and £12,000 per year.	

The *age allowances* have been increased for 1983/84 as fol-   **16**
lows:

single person	£2,360
married person	£3,755
income limit	£7,600

The limit for *mortgage interest relief* on your own home has   **18**
been increased to £30,000 for 1983/84.

The scheme for giving mortgage interest relief by deduction at source will be operative from 6th April 1983; all
borrowers affected by the change should have heard from
their building society or other lender about the new
arrangements.

The upper limit for higher rate tax relief for payments under   **22**
deeds of covenants to charities is increased to £5,000 for
1983/84 (see page 33).

The Inland Revenue have now introduced a standard
form of deed of covenant (called IR 47) for payments to
individuals.

The amount of the *widow's bereavement allowance* has been   **26**
increased to £1,010 for 1983/84. The allowance also applied
in the year following that in which the husband died, the
first such year being 1983/84.

Considerable interest has been aroused in a recent case   **41**
where a lady barrister successfully claimed a deduction for
tax purposes for the special clothes that she was required to
wear in court. It should be emphasised that the case is still
under appeal and that it has yet to be heard in the House of
Lords (the top appeal court); in any event, the facts of the
case were rather special and the Inland Revenue are likely to
resist strongly similar claims by other self-employed individuals.

53   The *small companies rate* of corporation tax for the year ended 31st March 1983 has been reduced to 38%; the full rate remains unchanged at 52%. The lower and upper limits for *marginal relief* have been raised to £100,000 and £500,000 respectively.

59   The lower rate of *corporation tax* is now 38%. An individual pays tax at 40% only when his taxable income exceeds £14,600, and at 55% when it exceeds £28,900.

61   The *ACT* rate for 1983/84 is unchanged at 3/7ths.

66   Changes in the legislation relating to overseas operations by companies are planned to come into force on 6th April 1984. These will apply particularly to overseas companies controlled by UK residents operating in low tax countries (the so-called 'tax havens').

67
76   The exemption limit for capital gains tax has been increased to £5,300 for 1983/84.
78

71   The exemption limit for capital gains tax on the let part of your home has been increased to £20,000 for 1983/84.

74   *Holdover relief* also applies now to assets transferred out of a trust, for example to a beneficiary.

81   The maximum amount of *retirement relief* has been increased to £100,000 for 1983/84 and thereafter.

The starting point for the payment of *capital transfer tax* has **83** been increased to £60,000 with effect from 15th March 1983.

The tables have also been amended with effect from the same date as follows:

Transfers made during your lifetime:
    Portion of value

Lower limit £	Upper limit £	Rate of tax %
nil	60,000	nil
60,000	80,000	15
80,000	110,000	17.5
110,000	140,000	20
140,000	175,000	22.5
175,000	220,000	25
220,000	270,000	30
270,000	700,000	35
700,000	1,325,000	40
1,325,000	2,650,000	45
2,650,000	–	50

Transfer made on death or within 3 years before:
    Portion of value

Lower limit £	Upper limit £	Rate Rate of tax %
nil	60,000	nil
60,000	80,000	30
80,000	110,000	35
110,000	140,000	40
140,000	175,000	45
175,000	220,000	50
220,000	270,000	55
270,000	700,000	60
700,000	1,325,000	65
1,325,000	2,650,000	70
2,650,000	–	75

87 The rate of interest on overdue capital transfer tax was reduced from 12% to 8% on lifetime and settled property transfers, and from 9% to 6% on transfers at death (or on additional tax due on a transfer made within three years of death), with effect from 1st December 1982.

90 The limit for transfers to a spouse who is not domiciled in the United Kingdom has been increased to £60,000 with effect from 15th March 1983.

For transfers to *charities*, the exemption limit of £250,000 for transfers made within 12 months prior to death has been abolished with effect from 15th March 1983.

92 For *business property relief* the reduction noted under **3** for non-controlling shareholdings in unquoted companies has been increased to 30% with effect from 15th March 1983.

For agricultural property relief, the reduction for let land has also been increased to 30% with effect from 15th March 1983.

98 The VAT *registration threshold* has been increased to £18,000 a year with effect from 16th March 1983.

99 The VAT *deregistration threshold* has been increased to £17,000 a year with effect from 1st June 1983.

101 The *business start-up scheme* has been significantly improved in the 1983 Budget. In particular the scheme is now to run until 5th April 1987 and the maximum amount allowable each year is increased to £40,000. It will also be amended so as to apply to investments in established unquoted trading companies as well as new ventures; for this reason the scheme has been renamed the *business expansion scheme*.

The *loan guarantee scheme* has also been extended, as have various special incentives for particular parts of the country.

Tax Return Checklist

These are the documents and information you will
need to have by you when filling in the tax form. If
you have an accountant, he will require all these
documents.

A Income	*Husband*	*Wife*

1   Employments, Directorships, etc.
Form P60 showing salary and tax
   deducted
Copy of form P11D, or details of
   expenses reimbursed by employer
Details of any company car used
   during the year (unless shown on
   form P11D)
Dates of absence from UK on overseas
   business trips
Details of any compensation payments
   for loss of office   _____ _____

Self-employment
Details of income and expenses, unless
   accounts are prepared separately   _____ _____

3   Pensions
National Insurance retirement pension
Widow's pension noting *current* weekly
   amounts
Other pensions/annuities from former
   employer   _____ _____

4   Property
Income receivable
Expenses incurred – receipts where
   available
   Distinguish between furnished
   and unfurnished lettings   _____ _____

5   Untaxed interest received
Bank deposit accounts
Trustee Savings Bank Accounts

		Husband	*Wife*
	National Savings Bank Accounts (specifying whether ordinary or investment accounts) Government Stocks Tax Deposit Certificates Any other untaxed interest	_____	_____
6	**Building Society interest received**	_____	_____
7	**Taxed income** Dividends Trust Income Annuities Loan Stock Any other taxed income Supply counterfoils/vouchers/tax deduction certificates	_____	_____
8	**Foreign income** Earnings Any other income Supply certificates showing foreign and/or UK tax deducted where possible	_____	_____
9	**Children's Income (under 18)**	_____	_____
10	**Single Premium Life Bonds** Details of purchases Details of withdrawals, encashments, surrenders and disposals	_____	_____
11	**Any Other Income** Commission Casual earnings Any other income not covered elsewhere	_____	_____
B	**Outgoings**		
1	**Expenses** Professional subscriptions Other expenses claimable against earnings	_____	_____

		Husband	*Wife*
2	**Interest paid** Mortgage interest Loan interest Bank interest	_____	_____
3	**Maintenance Payments, Alimony, etc.**	_____	_____
4	**Deeds of covenant** Supply date of deed, amounts paid and to whom payable.	_____	_____
5	**Reitrement annuities** Supply details of premiums paid and forms SEPC for new policies.	_____	_____
6	**Life assurance policies** Supply details of any changes	_____	_____
C	**Capital**		
1	**Stocks and shares** Supply details of acquisitions and disposals with contract notes	_____	_____
2	**Other assets** Supply details of any acquisitions and disposals *including* main residence.	_____	_____
3	**Transfers of value received or made** Supply details of any legacies or gifts received or made.	_____	_____
D	**General**		
1	**Personal circumstances** Any changes likely to affect your tax position or claim for allowances.	_____	_____
2	**Date of birth** Husband Wife	_____	_____
3	**Any other information** that may be relevant to the completion of the tax return.	_____	_____